GW00598034

RETRO AND VINTAGE BOATS

RETRO AND VINTAGE BOATS

Kiwi Portraits

Don Jessen

Bateman

DEDICATION

This book is dedicated in loving memory
to my dad, Eric 'Tek' Rushlee Jessen, and my son, Zaan Rushlee Jessen,
and to all like-minded Kiwis who just love mucking around in boats.

Text © Don Jessen, 2015
Design and typography © David Bateman Ltd, 2015

Published in 2015 by David Bateman Ltd
30 Tarndale Grove, Albany, Auckland, New Zealand

www.batemanpublishing.co.nz

A catalogue record for this book is available from the National Library of New Zealand.

ISBN 978-1-86953-896-5

This book is copyright. Except for the purpose of fair review, no part may be stored or transmitted in any
form or by any means, electronic or mechanical, including recording or storage in any information retrieval
systems, without permission in writing from the publisher. No reproduction may be made, whether by
photocopying or by any other means, unless a licence has been obtained from the publisher or its agent.

Publisher: Bill Honeybone
Book design: Cheryl Smith, Macarn Design
All images by Marilyn Jessen (including front and back covers), except for those by the author
(pages 27, 98–101, 206–7, 220–21, 242 [top left and right]), from the Jessen Family Archives (page 116),
Deidi Duncan (page 177), and from individual boat owners (pages 38–9, 82–3, 96–7, 134–5, 138 [right],
139 [top], 154–7 and 198–9).
Printed in China by Asia Pacific Offset Ltd

Contents

Introduction

As a kid, I was brought up on a diet of caravans and small trailer boats. My dad was a mad keen boatie and built his first 10-foot (3 m) boat in 1950. A 12-footer (3.7 m) followed in 1955, with a 14-foot (4.3 m) cabin boat replacing that in 1959. That year I also got my first boat for Christmas: an 8-foot (2.4 m) pram dinghy.

As it was in those days, the average Kiwi boatie tended to run small open boats or small cabin boats up to about 17 foot (5.2 m), powered by either a marinised car engine, or an outboard motor. Outboard motors tended to range from 4 hp Seagulls to giant 33 hp and 40 hp Scott-Atwaters, Mercurys or Johnsons. Over the years, the size of these boats would generally increase as the owners were able to afford to upgrade.

As readers of my first book, *Retro Caravans: Vantastic Kiwi Collections*, will know, I am passionate about old caravans and cars. What many do not realise, though, is that I also love retro motorcycles and boats! My lifelong love of boats can be traced back to my dad and those great days of the 1950s. At the age of

nine, I considered myself to be something of an expert when it came to boats. I would devour Dad's American boat magazines and, when available, New Zealand's own *Sea Spray* magazine. I became familiar with the terms 'clinker', 'runabout', 'cabin cruiser', 'speedboat' and 'launch'. In respect of the latter, the words 'bridgedecker', 'flushdecker', 'tram-top' and 'sedan' became part of my nautical vocabulary. With schoolboy authority I reeled off designers' names like John Spencer, Carl Augustin, Jim Young, Richard Hartley, Sam Ford, Col Wild and, of course, the Logan Brothers.

By the time I got to 18 my dad had progressed to a fibreglass runabout and, once I was 21, I bought my first speedboat. She had been built in 1955 and had probably been powered by a Ford 10 motor. By the time I got her she was powered by a 1500 Cortina GT motor. It was the beginning of a string of 12 boats that I would own, the largest being a 42-footer (12.8 m).

Along with my dad and another Liteweight Caravans staff

member, I designed a number of different-sized aluminium boats that we then built and sold under the Liteweight brand from 1986 to 1990. In all, we built 278 boats.

When I started on this book I believed myself to be quite knowledgeable about boats. As I progressed, I came to realise that my knowledge was rather generalised. I have met owners who have a great in-depth knowledge of their particular craft — far greater than I will ever have. I also came to learn just how vast the topic of retro/vintage/replica boats is, and also how many of these craft exist in New Zealand. We have an incredibly rich maritime history and many old boats are alive and well and still plying our coasts and inland lakes. So many that I believe I could write five such books and still not cover them all.

Having myself been a trailer boatie, a yachtie, and a launch owner during my boating career, I can really appreciate all these boats, from the smallest sailing craft to trailer boats, speedboats and lovely launches.

There has been an awful lot written about historic boats in New Zealand and some of them are pretty famous locally, particularly some of the yachts and old bridgedecker launches, however I found myself more interested in the older, and replica, boats that are not so well known. I came away from my various 'research voyages' with well over 100 boats photographed. When I looked through them a week or so later, I realised that here indeed were the beginnings of a great compendium of retro and vintage boats.

The book is split into sections of some of the different types of boats to be found in our coastal and inland waters, from the time-honoured clinkers and picnic boats, steam launches, runabouts, cabin cruisers, jet boats and speedboats of our earlier years, to a small selection of vintage and replica launches. At the end of the book there is a selection of photographs of other boats and boating scenes that caught my eye and so they, too, have been included.

One thing that all the boats have in common is that their owners lavish a lot of attention on them. Some of the craft are so historically significant that the owners consider themselves caretakers of the boat's life voyage. And don't just think it's the man of the family who has the interest. I've come across many women who are just as passionate about their old boats.

Some of the boats are, in my opinion, absolute gems. Some have fascinating histories while others' histories have been lost. Some of them have gorgeous lines, others are quaint, slow, or very quick. Some are old, others very old, and still others are new but look old. Hopefully, there is something of interest to all you boaties out there.

I have greatly enjoyed putting this book together and have been amazed at the warmth of boat owners' responses and their willingness to share what they know about their boats. I hope that I have done justice to the boats featured and have produced a book that you, the reader, will find both interesting and enjoyable.

The Iconic Clinker

As a young lad in the '50s, I remember visiting coastal motor camps where open boats from 8 to 14 foot (2.4 to 4.3 m) littered the beaches and tidal areas. There was always at least one clinker sitting on the sand or floating in the tide.

The word 'clinker', or description 'clinker-built', defines a style of boat or boatbuilding where the edges of the external planks of the boat overlap downwards and are secured with clinched nails. It is a very strong type of construction.

The earliest evidence of a clinker-style boat are fragments found in an archaeological excavation site in modern-day Denmark, and which date back to the Iron Age (around 200 to 400 AD). Viking longships were built using this style of construction so it is clear this is a very traditional way of boat building.

The oldest clinker I have come across in New Zealand was built in 1895, though it is probable that earlier clinker-style boats were built here. Many of the boats were built as work boats, as tenders for gold dredges, as small steam launches or sailers for navigating passengers up rivers and estuaries to settlements, or, in some cases, for coastal travel.

At a later date they started to be used as tenders to scows, yachts and launches. The earlier versions often tended to have small inboard motors. By the 1950s there was a noticeable move in New Zealand to power clinkers and other ply dinghies with small outboard motors. By the late '60s/early '70s, boat manufacturers were taking moulds off existing clinker boats and reproducing them in fibreglass.

The boats featured here are the genuine article, all constructed in timber. They are made for different uses, with different fit-outs, but all are unmistakably clinkers!

Stiffy

1947–48

Owner Harold

My wife spotted this lovely clinker-designed Frostbite sailing dinghy and dragged me across to have a look at it. Painted in a beautiful aqua colour, it certainly looked very nice. No one is quite sure how she was named but she has been *Stiffy* for a long time. She still has her original Yachting New Zealand registration number: 122. Her length is 11 ft 6 in (3.5 m), and she carries a beam of 4 ft 10 in (1.5 m). The sail area is 72 square feet (6.7 square metres).

The design apparently originated in 1938, with the designer named as Jack Brooke. She was built by RF Bright in Devonport, Auckland, in 1947/48 and launched in 1948. *Stiffy* is believed to have had only three owners, one of which was the Papatoetoe Sea Rangers, before Harold acquired her in 1988.

He has enjoyed the yacht for many years, and in Picton in 2006 fully restored her to her current state.

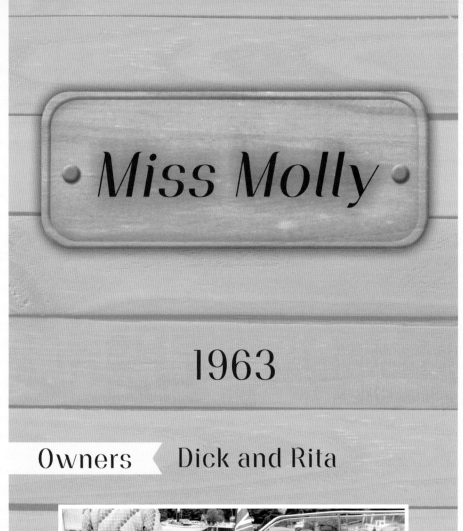

Miss Molly

1963

Owners Dick and Rita

Good golly, Miss Molly, what a sweet-looking clinker runabout you are! There is a symmetry to your hull shape. Your deck and screen are well balanced, giving a very pleasing look overall. They tell me you were built by Mahan Boat Company, in the Redcliffs area of Christchurch in 1963.

Dick and Rita Hall purchased *Miss Molly* in January 2014 from a retired doctor in Temuka, whose family had used her for many years for outings from their crib at 'Kaik', just south of Moeraki. Initially powered by a 1963 15 hp Johnson outboard, she was later fitted with a 1972 20 hp Mercury outboard to allow her to get up on the plane with four people aboard, primarily to beat the weather home should it turn nasty. At the time of Dick and Rita's purchase the Mercury motor was reputed to have had less than 30 hours' running time! Barely run in.

When I first saw *Miss Molly*, I found her very appealing. She looked so beautiful with her varnished decks and clinker hull. I understand from Dick and Rita that she was a little run down when they acquired her, but a winter restoration, including sanding back her hull and decks and re-varnishing, soon fixed her up.

Dick has a rather wonderful tow car, a 1955 Studebaker Champion, that he takes to classic shows, with *Miss Molly* hooked on behind. Dick and Rita have become members of the Picton Clinker and Classic Boating Club and, together with *Miss Molly*, use the Marlborough Sounds and the Nelson Lakes as their playground.

Fiddler's Green

Circa 1930s–'40s

Owner ⟩ Stephen

This sweet little ketch has borne the name *Fiddler's Green* since 1976. Before that it is understood that she did not actually have a name. She was likely built in the 1930s or '40s as a motor launch, with decking, cockpit and a stand-up cabin, and powered by an inboard motor with tiller steer.

As a launch she would have been used for fishing and access to cribs/baches, most likely in the Abel Tasman area, as for many years she was seen moored in the local tidal estuaries and bays of the area.

The boat is of solid construction and quality craftsmanship, which has certainly stood the test of time. It was these strong characteristics that led to the boat being recovered from neglect in 1976 and converted into a ketch, then named *Fiddler's Green*. The inboard motor was removed and the cabin cut down. A heavy keel was cast and fitted. Wooden masts and rigging were scavenged from another derelict yacht, and new sails were made by Landsmeer Sails in Christchurch. The main and mizzen sails are gaff rigged with a jib to the fore. In 1982, a 7.5 hp Evinrude outboard was added.

Fiddler's Green is 14 feet (4.3 m) LOA (length overall) with a 5 ft 6 in (1.7 m) beam. She has a draught of 2 ft 7 in (0.8 m). In the 1990s, the hull and deck were stripped of paint. She also benefited from new framing timber, ribs and a new deck and cabin. She was also repainted throughout.

In 2011/12 she again underwent a refit, with her paint being stripped back to bare timber and repainted. New varnish was completed on the deck areas, the brassware was polished and clear-coat lacquered. A new trailer was built to take *Fiddler's Green* on new adventures. Throughout these refits, the original masts, rigging and sails were retained and are still in excellent condition.

This is a stunning little clinker ketch (the smallest I have ever seen) and, under sail, she makes such a pretty picture.

Blue Duck

1895

Owners Peter and Angela

This very old 1895 fantail clinker has a remarkable history. She was built by the Knewstubb brothers in Port Chalmers as an oil launch tender for one of the many gold dredgers used on the Shotover and other rivers. The current owners possess a very old photo showing her tied up to a dredge. The word 'fantail' refers to the shape of the stern, which resembles the tail of the bird.

Blue Duck has been a motor-powered boat all her life, probably having sported three or four different motors at different times, judging by the number of exhaust holes found at the time of her restoration. When the current owners found her, they discovered that the original bronze stern tube was still in her, but had been cut off flush with the hull both inside and outside, and plugged at both ends. It is believed she may have had another plank on the freeboard when first built as there were no deck fittings in the original stern and the top has adze markings that are still visible.

Sometime in the 1950s or '60s she was converted to a keeler. Another 300 mm and a lump of railway iron were added to the keel and another plank to the topsides, along with a cabin. This was all held together with galvanised nails skewed down into the sheer clamp and transom, with bits of copper sheeting wrapped around them. She was glassed with polyester, which caused some problems as one of the starboard planks buckled and cracked due to uneven moisture levels, causing her to sink at her mooring in Frankton Arm, Lake Wakatipu. She was recovered and transported to Cromwell were she lay on the hard for 15 years. She was then transported to Alexandra where she suffered the ultimate insult for a working boat: becoming a garden ornament for a further 10 years.

How did Peter come across this boat? An item on his wish-list was to restore an old boat and make it a steamer. He posted his wish on the Internet and was contacted by the owner. Peter could not believe his luck. Not only was this a clinker hull with a history, but a very rare fantail stern model — something so rare that not too many boat builders would have the skills to build it.

So began the restoration, from garden ornament to a historic steam launch. Peter and his dad, Paul, restored the hull and converted her to a steamer. She is now powered by a Hasbrook 2½ hp diesel-fired boiler, which takes 20 minutes to get to full working pressure. Cruising speed is 5 knots at 180 rpm.

I asked Peter how she got her name. The story goes that once he had restored the boat he had her on display and an old fellow wandered up and asked him if it was 'Blue Duck'. Peter thought the old fellow seemed so certain that he named the boat then and there.

She now looks an absolute picture under way, particularly with the tiny 1910 clinker dinghy in tow. The restoration is a credit to Peter and his dad.

Blue Duck's Little One

Blue Duck's tender is a 5 ft 6 in (1.7 m) clinker built in 1910. It has a kauri hull and was found in the Otaki tip in 2003, then restored by Peter with new top planks, ribs and seats. Whoever built this wee boat knew what they were doing and must have been a very skilled boat builder to get the kauri timber to bend around such tight curves. For such a small boat you would have to be able to select the right timber, cut it just right, then steam it to just the right temperature and moisture content so that when it cools and dries off it stays just where you put it, and won't break or split as you bend it.

Peter took three months of searching all over the lower North Island before he found the recycled kauri planks that had just the right grain and cut profile. Like *Blue Duck*, *Little One* is beautifully restored and a true credit to Peter's dedication to the task.

Keeper

Circa 1957

Owner Dave

Dave lives in Kaiapoi, just north of Christchurch, and for many years his family hired a crib at Duncan Bay, Pelorus Sound. For the 20 years they went there, a clinker dinghy lay under cover on the section. As far as Dave could tell, it had never moved.

Eventually, the owner died and the widow decided to sell the property. Dave asked her what she was going to do with the old clinker, and told her he thought it could be restored. She told him he could have the boat so Dave rounded up some friends and shot up to the crib, picked up the boat, and returned to Kaiapoi — all in one weekend.

He spent the next few months restoring the boat, and his son, Todd, took on the job of restoring the old outboard. The motor was a 10 hp Johnson of around 1957 vintage and Todd was able to import motor parts and decals from the US. Once restored mechanically, Dave painted it in its original colours, then Todd fitted the decals and handgrips to finish it.

Dave wonders whether the hull was modified at some time from a displacement to a planing hull, as the bottom is pretty flat and she has quite a reasonable tumblehome. She certainly gets up and planes quite well with the 10 hp Johnson.

I notice a mint 5½ hp Scott-Atwater outboard of about the same vintage sitting next to *Keeper* and ask Dave about it. They imported it from the States and Dave is quite delighted when I tell him that back in the '50s my dad had a 7½ hp version that looked identical to his.

The Smoke Boats (Steam Launches)

It came as something of a surprise to me when I came across a good number of steam launches on a North Island lake and, later, on a South Island lake. I have to say that they fascinated me from the first look, in particular the fastidious detail on each boat and the intricacies of the engines and boilers.

These boats generally are a work of art. Featured here are seven steam launches, ranging from the open picnic launch style to the fully cabined river/lake-style day boat. Each is unique in its own way, so sit back and let yourself be transported back to a time when steam ruled.

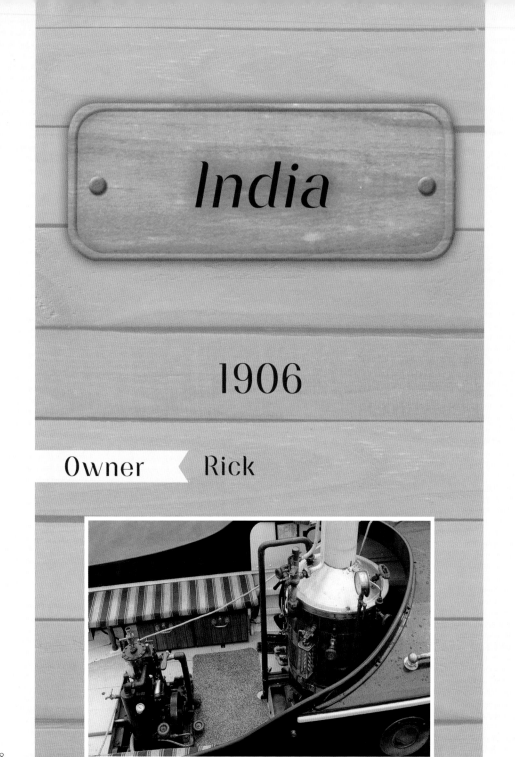

India

1906

Owner Rick

This 22-foot (6.7 m) coal-burning steam launch was built by Hobbs boat builders of Whangaparaoa and launched in 1906. It was built for Bill Shakespeare, who was apprenticed to the Logan Brothers, and was believed to be related to the Hobbs family. *India* has a beam of 5 ft 6 in (1.7 m), and is constructed of double-skin kauri, with a pohutukawa transom, knees and belting. The current owner, Rick, is her fifth owner and lives in Renwick.

Originally, *India* was built as an open boat with an oil engine and a spritsail rig, similar to a gaff rig. The cabin was added in 1922. The boiler is a vertical fire tube design by Stuart Turner and was built by McKenzie and Ridley in 1988, in Auckland. She has a working pressure of 100 psi. The engine design was drawn in 1944 by OB Bolton in Sydney, Australia, and she was built by John Bow in Auckland.

For those in the know, the engine has a bore three-inch (7.6 cm) and a stroke four-inch (10 cm) double acting. For those of us with little mechanical knowledge, this is probably double Dutch. The 18 x 24-inch (46 x 61 cm) propeller gives a speed of approximately 6 knots at 300 rpm. Although not generally a steam boat type of guy, I have to admit they intrigue me. They have such beautiful lines and the workmanship and the quality restorations are impressive, further complemented by the astonishing motors and boilers, which are unique to each boat.

India is no exception to the rule. She is just plain beautiful to look at.

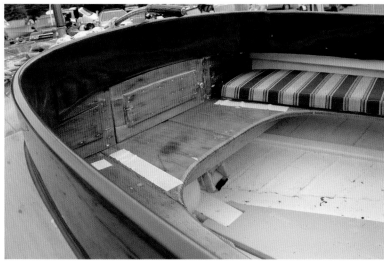

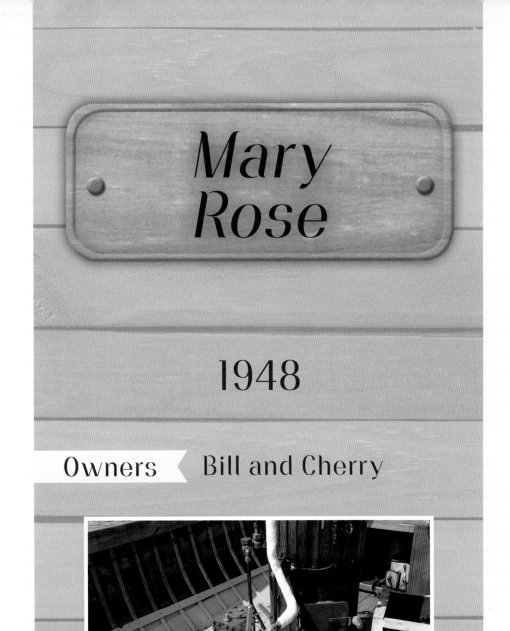

Mary Rose

1948

Owners Bill and Cherry

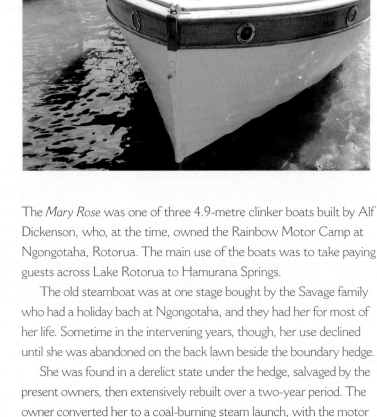

The *Mary Rose* was one of three 4.9-metre clinker boats built by Alf Dickenson, who, at the time, owned the Rainbow Motor Camp at Ngongotaha, Rotorua. The main use of the boats was to take paying guests across Lake Rotorua to Hamurana Springs.

The old steamboat was at one stage bought by the Savage family who had a holiday bach at Ngongotaha, and they had her for most of her life. Sometime in the intervening years, though, her use declined until she was abandoned on the back lawn beside the boundary hedge.

She was found in a derelict state under the hedge, salvaged by the present owners, then extensively rebuilt over a two-year period. The owner converted her to a coal-burning steam launch, with the motor and boiler made by W Larsen. The motor is a single-cylinder unit.

The boat was awarded the prize for 'Best Boat' in the 2004 Wooden Boat Parade on Lake Rotoiti, where she is still based, and is now a regular 'lady of the lake'.

Like many of the steam launches in this chapter, she is in immaculate condition and I was thoroughly taken with her lines, the highly polished brass work, and the aesthetics of the engine and boiler. I can't say I would ever aspire to own one, largely due to the ongoing work involved, but I can certainly admire the beauty of them.

SS *Flirt*

Owners ⟩ Bob and Sue

This boat has a big history. She is a combination of two steam launches, both named *Flirt*. The original *Flirt* was commissioned in 1894 for a customer in British Columbia, Canada. The company chosen was Simpson Strickland in Dartmouth, England. With a production number of 376, she was built with a double-planked mahogany hull. Her engine was a Simpson Strickland Kingdon AB with a Kingdon fire tube boiler, which ran about 125 pounds of steam pressure at 450 rpm, producing 14 hp and a speed of 9 mph.

Flirt was shipped across the Atlantic, slung on a passenger ship's lifeboat davit. From there she progressed by rail to a Canadian lake, and was then carried by a sternwheeler vessel a further 200 miles (321 km) up the lake, before embarking on another rail trip to her final destination. Once on the lake, in 1896, she was commissioned into service with the Balfour Steam Navigation Company.

In 1903, a boating club was formed on the lake, with owner Charles Busk becoming its first commodore. Little is known of *Flirt* after this date until she was sold in 1917. She was again sold in 1925 to John Nelson. Many years later, son Walter Nelson sold her to a Mr Tennyson. He lived in a boat and thought he might use *Flirt's* engine in it. When he discovered that the engine had a cracked cylinder head and would need a boiler and coal to make it go, he immediately on-sold it to Joe Higgs. He had built a 16 ft 8 in (5.1 m) hull in the 1950s and had named her *Flirt* after the original *Flirt* he had once admired. Joe's *Flirt* had an open round bottom, carvel-planked

displacement hull, which was made of a combination of oak, red cedar, copper, brass and iron. Carvel planking is a method of construction where the planks are fastened edge to edge, gaining support from the frame, and forming a smooth surface. The shape was reminiscent of 1930s design. *Flirt*'s funnel, wine glass tumblehome stern, and brass whistle belong to a much earlier time.

In 2006, Joe's *Flirt* was advertised for sale and, after due diligence, the newer *Flirt* hull and lots of fittings from the original *Flirt* were shipped to New Zealand. On arrival, an assessment was made under the watchful eye of Bruce Askew, a renowned naval architect. It was decided that the hull needed considerable work to make her seaworthy and that the engine grossly overloaded the boat. With this in mind, plans were sourced from a British museum of a similar-sized boat built by Simpson Strickland. These plans were redrawn to fit New Zealand towing widths

and scaled to an 8 m length to fit with bylaws on length for New Zealand lakes.

Flirt was rebuilt using a single carvel-planked hull of white pine with white oak ribs. The keel is a mixture of kauri and macrocarpa, and the cabin and deck are teak. A new cylinder was made, with the cracked cylinder from the original *Flirt* used as a back-up. The original *Flirt* had plans supplied for the boiler and was the basis for a new build, carried out by Whangaparaoa's Colonial Iron Works Co. Ltd, who added modern safety and construction features but retained the traditional coal-burning capacity.

Flirt was relaunched on 5 March 2011 at St Arnaud, and now steams around the lake. She is a stunning old steam launch, encompassing English, Canadian and New Zealand boating history. She has a lake boat-style cabin and can carry a good number of passengers.

Clansman

2011 (1900 replica)

Owner Tim

Clansman is a replica steam launch based on the *Lady Elizabeth*, a steamboat in the collection of the Windermere Steam Boat Museum in the UK. The plans for *Clansman* were drawn by marine draughtsman Sean Booth.

Construction on *Clansman* started in 2000 and was completed in early 2011. Her length is 5.9 m and her beam 1.8 m. A combination of traditional and modern boat-building techniques, the hull is built in 14 mm strip-plank kauri and sheathed inside and out in biaxial glass cloth. The deck is 12 mm ply with overlaid 8 mm Iroko sheathing and ash seams.

The engine is a 5 hp Compound with the boiler a 20 square foot (1.9 square metre) Blackstaff. Departing from tradition, it is diesel-fired via a steam-atomising burner. The engineering work was carried out by Gavin Fazakerley from Parua Bay in Whangarei.

After a phase of dealing with a few teething issues, *Clansman* is going really well and getting plenty of use, both in Northland waters and on the inland lakes of New Zealand.

I am always amazed at how much knowledge the owners have about the build and also the engine and boiler specifications. I have to admit to scratching my head a bit when they list the mechanical details, so don't feel bad if you do too. It doesn't stop me from being drawn to them. There is a real sense of romance as these boats cross the lake with smoke issuing from the stack, and I'm always impressed by their quietness. A very peaceful way to go boating.

Romany

1994 (1880s plan)

Owner Russell

Romany provided my introduction to steam launches, and I was hugely impressed by her elegance and the sense of a bygone era she invoked.

You could be forgiven for thinking that I had made a mistake on the build year by at least 100 years, but *Romany* is actually a replica boat, modelled on a working launch of the 1880s, but built in 1994. She was initially built by Alec Butler who, unfortunately, died just before the hull was completed. The present owner finished the project, and the boat is an absolute credit to both men.

She is 5.6 m long, and has been traditionally constructed in a very heavy work-boat style, with a hardwood keel, spotted gum ribs and copper-fastened kauri planking. *Romany* runs a coal-fired steam engine, which is a single-cylinder unit. Ten pounds of coal provides fuel for around an hour, and it takes half an hour to raise enough steam from cold. Steam boating is by its very nature an act of patience.

Vital Spark

1986 replica

Owner Peter

Vital Spark has a GRP (Glass-Reinforced Plastic), or fibreglass, hull and was built in 1986 by Steam & Electric Launch Co. at Wroxham, England, to a Rupert Lantham design known as the Frolic 21. She was then shipped to Hong Kong where she was fitted out by Regatta Yachts. The boiler was built, also in 1986, by Langley Engineering in England and is known as a Kingdon type VFT. The engine is a Stuart Turner, built in 1979.

The boat first steamed up in February 1988 and was owned by a gentleman by the name of Myron Givets, and registered with the Hong Kong Yacht Club. She was shipped to New Zealand in June 1996 and acquired by Peter in 2000. Peter replaced the original Stuart Turner engine in 2003.

Vital Spark's vital statistics give a length of 21 feet (6.4 m), with a waterline length of 19 ft 6 in (5.9 m). Her beam is 5 ft 8 in (1.7 m) and her draught 1 ft 11 in (0.6 m). She has a white hull, gold boot-top stripe at the waterline and blue undersides, with a stunning varnished teak deck and interior.

Vital Spark looks very smart with her traditional-looking hull, sporting a counter stern, and her unusual surrey top cabin. Every attention has been paid to the details, from the centre steering position and fittings to the rounded timberwork fore and aft. The cabin is fitted with clear awnings to enclose the space for inclement weather. Peter tends to use her around New Zealand lakes and thoroughly enjoys the boat. I love the name Vital Spark — it seems so appropriate for a steam launch.

SS *Eliza Hobson*

1996 (1880s plan)

Owners ▸ **Doug and Maria**

Doug and Maria have lived for a long time in a beautifully restored villa on the banks of the Waikato River, with their lawn running gently to the river's edge. Moored at the bottom of the lawn is the beautiful replica 30-foot (9.1 m) steamboat *Eliza Hobson*. What a stunning-looking boat, and in such a picturesque mooring site! So what is this boat doing on the Waikato River?

Doug likes old things and when he saw the boat for sale on Trade Me two years ago, he had to have it. The owner came down and viewed the river setting and agreed it was the right place for her to be. Doug and Maria used her for cruising the river, until an unfortunate incident cracked the boiler. At the time the photographs were taken, the boiler was out being repaired.

So what about her previous life?

She was built in 1996 as a replica steam launch of the 1880s, incorporating all the best features of that bygone era. Owned by Alan and Sue Lambourne, *Eliza Hobson* operated out of the Viaduct basin in Auckland, taking passengers on trips out on the harbour. The high cost of berthage caused them to relocate to the Kerikeri Inlet, travelling up the coast in the boat to get there. From Kerikeri she continued her life as a tourist boat, taking passengers on river trips.

She is built out of kauri and totara, and has a vertical fire tube boiler.

Picnic Boats

Picnic boats are known by a variety of names, including 'settler boats', 'day boats', 'river boats' and 'lake boats', and were among the first type of powered craft in this fair country of ours. In general, the boats' chief purpose was for informal outings, largely on calm and protected waters. They were used, as the names suggests, for day trips to islands for picnics, or for river and lake travel that did not require overnighting. All of them are displacement boats, some are open boats, and others have cabin styles, as depicted in the following pages.

Although not trailerable in their day, many of them are now trailered, moving from one location to another, for added convenience. They generally range in length from 16 to 26 feet (4.9 to 7.9 m). I had not seen this style of early settler boat much before so I am very grateful to the people who have restored or built replicas of these great boats as they preserve a very important part of our maritime heritage.

Firefly

1882

Owners   Allan and Ronda

This boat is reputed to be the oldest launch still in operation in New Zealand. She was built north of Auckland in 1882 and although designed as a picnic boat, it is likely she was used to ferry supplies to farms and nearby islands. Midway through last century, she was used as a work boat on Lake Manapouri when the power station was under construction. It is believed that she has never had a sail fitted and has always been a powered craft.

Firefly is a 25-foot (7.6 m) counter stern launch. Her original name has been lost over time, with her current name chosen by a previous owner. She is known to have had six different motors over her lifetime, including at least two steam engines, and was still steam-powered when the current owner bought her in Coromandel. *Firefly* is currently powered by a Stuart Turner two-cylinder, two-stroke petrol engine, giving her a cruising speed of 5 knots. She has very pretty lines and was completely restored in 2008.

With her beautiful woodwork and cane chairs, *Firefly* conjures up visions of elegant ladies in long dresses and wide-brimmed hats held on by lengthy scarves, when the main event of the day was a genteel picnic on the foreshore. Currently domiciled on Lake Rotoiti (Rotorua), *Firefly* is deservedly known as the 'Grand Old Lady of the Lake'.

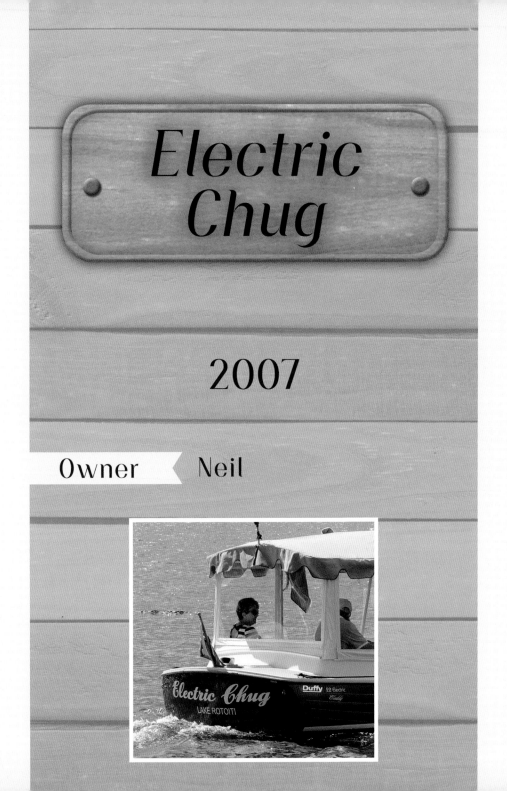

Electric Chug

2007

Owner Neil

Electric Chug is a fibreglass replica of an American design, based on the lake picnic boats of yesteryear. She has a length of 22 feet (6.7 m) and a beam of 9 ft 3 in (2.8 m). She is incredibly roomy, able to carry 12 adults comfortably, and comes complete with a canvas surrey top.

There is, however, one major difference with this replica picnic boat, and that is the motive power. Throw away the steam engine, the diesel and the petrol engine, this beauty is electrically powered. There is a bank of batteries under the floor, running along the keel. These are connected to a small electric motor (this explains her name!) that sits on top of the rudder. At the base and rear of the rudder blade is the propeller. The positioning of the propeller on the rudder blade allows *Electric Chug* to turn on her axis. She cruises at 7 knots, and a full charge will last seven and a half hours. She runs a trickle charge system and, back at the boat shed, she simply gets plugged in. Her owner, Neil, reports that she works perfectly and he has had no problems with her.

The question I have for Neil is how he ended up with an electric-powered boat.

Neil had been looking for a classic launch, but being extremely busy he wanted something low-maintenance but with classic looks. He went on the net and found the American boat, then discovered they were available ex-Australia, where a number of them are used in and around Sydney Harbour and on the Gold Coast as tourist boats. A quick trip to Aussie, a ride in one of the tourist boats, and Neil was sold. *Electric Chug* is a 2007 model and is powered by a modern, efficient electric motor. Neil uses her for day boating and fishing. It is uncanny as you 'hear' her go silently past you!

Caravel

1962

Owner Richard

Caravel was built in 1962 by Norm Keen for the late Chip Stevens of Hauparu Bay.

She is of kauri-planked (carvel) construction with teak decks and a mahogany cabin, and is still powered by the original 75 hp Volvo Penta BB70 petrol engine that has amassed a grand total of around 1700 hours from new.

The requirements of the design were to style her after the Thames (England) police launches of the 1950s, and the criteria included that the engine did not encroach on the cabin space. She had to accommodate guests either sitting in the cabin or the cockpit without any undue changes in trim. Her dimensions were limited by the existing boat shed and cradle.

Norm, a master craftsman, created this beautiful example of traditional boat building at his boatyard in Okawa Bay during the winter of 1962. She was launched on Christmas Eve and has been a familiar sight on the lake ever since. She still remains in the family.

Otira

1901

Owner   Tino Rawa Trust

Otira is an original picnic boat, built in 1901. Her condition is amazing, and she looks a much younger boat than she is. The Tino Rawa Trust is a registered charity created in 2007 to assist in the 'preservation, restoration and caretaking of New Zealand's unique classic yacht and launch heritage'. A significant aspect of the trust's work is education, and many initiatives are aimed at involving youth in New Zealand's sailing heritage. *Otira* is one of many boats owned by the trust, and was donated in 2012 by Paul Pritchett, who had restored her between 2005 and 2007.

Otira was designed and built by the famed Logan Brothers and measures 20 feet (6.1 m) overall. Originally, she sported a cabin and dodger (giving protection from spray), which were removed as part of the restoration. The hull was refastened to the original frame with copper nails, the old paint was removed by burning it off, and rotten timbers were replaced with recycled kauri. Because the jarrah and pohutukawa outer stem, keel and dead wood (the lower part of the boat's stem or stern) had worn, these were replaced by new hardwood, and the caulking was removed and replaced with a compound to seal the joints. Coamings were steam-bent and varnished to bring her up to today's glory with her beautifully polished woodwork. The original brass fairleads, bollard and rudder were all retained. At the time of restoration she was powered by a Stuart diesel marine engine, however this was later replaced with a new inboard Lombardini 502 20 hp motor to improve handling, reliability and safety.

It is fantastic that the trust is preserving these boats for us to enjoy.

Sarah Hutton

2002 replica (1900 plan)

Owner Tino Rawa Trust

At a Lake Rotoiti Classic and Wooden Boat Association Parade and Picnic I attended, the *Otira* (see page 60) lay next to this, the *Sarah Hutton*, another picnic launch of similar dimensions and style. The parade is held in February each year, and boats from all over the North Island participate, including the resident local Lake Rotoiti boats. It is well worth the trip to watch the parade from the Okere arm of the lake, and many drivers on their trip to Tauranga pause to enjoy the visual spectacle and listen to the commentary.

The *Sarah Hutton* is a replica trailerable picnic launch built in 2002, and, when seen next to her sister boat *Otira* (built in 1901), it is hard to tell which boat is the oldest. *Sarah Hutton* is also owned by the Tino Rawa Trust, but was built 101 years after *Otira*. In design and overall condition, however, you could not pick the difference. Like the *Otira*, *Sarah Hutton* is immaculate in her presentation.

Sarah Hutton was designed and built by Robert Brooke in 2002, and I take my hat off to him. She is a superb boat. Her specifications are: length 5 m; beam 2.25 m; and draught a shallow 400 mm. She was built from New Zealand kauri in traditional clinker fashion and runs a 13 hp Lombardini engine.

She was originally built for an American superyacht owner as a toy. After paying for it and asking the builder to store it until he was able to take delivery, the owner then decided not to bother with it and left it in New Zealand. She is now used in coastal waters around Auckland for cruising and general enjoyment, as well as for historic regattas and exhibitions.

Relax-Ay-Voo

1997

Owner John

Relax-Ay-Voo was built and launched in 1997 after John, the owner, spent several years searching unsuccessfully for a good lake boat. John sketched up some ideas of what he thought would be a good boat and took them to designer Bruce Askew. With all the boats John had looked at, he had developed two pet hates: many of the older boats had a hulking great motor in the cabin, taking up a huge amount of room, and most of the boats were small on cockpit space.

John's specification to Bruce was for clear floor space in the cabin, and a large cockpit area. Bruce designed the 8 m boat as a displacement launch with a small 30 hp diesel Volvo motor situated up in the bow running a fairly flat propeller shaft, which also meant the boat did not draw too much depth. The cabin was open plan and a large cockpit was built. The hull was built in kauri plank and traditionally fastened with copper nails. It was then splined and fibreglassed over. The topsides were built in teak and mahogany. The panoramic window configuration and surrey top roof, along with the stunning woodwork and twin steering station, make this an incredibly pretty and practical boat.

John and his family have clocked up 3500 hours in *Relax-Ay-Voo* and are rather famous for their all-day cruises and night cruising. The boat burns 2.5 litres per hour and cruises at a comfortable 7 knots. To quote John: 'We enjoy going nowhere slowly.' Not quite true, as they often visit friends in the evening by boat rather than car. The family also owns a ski boat so the kids take the ski boat to a bay for a day's skiing, with *Relax-Ay-Voo* anchored nearby as the mother ship. This boat really sounds like a member of the family.

Whitney

2012

Owners Colin and Dale

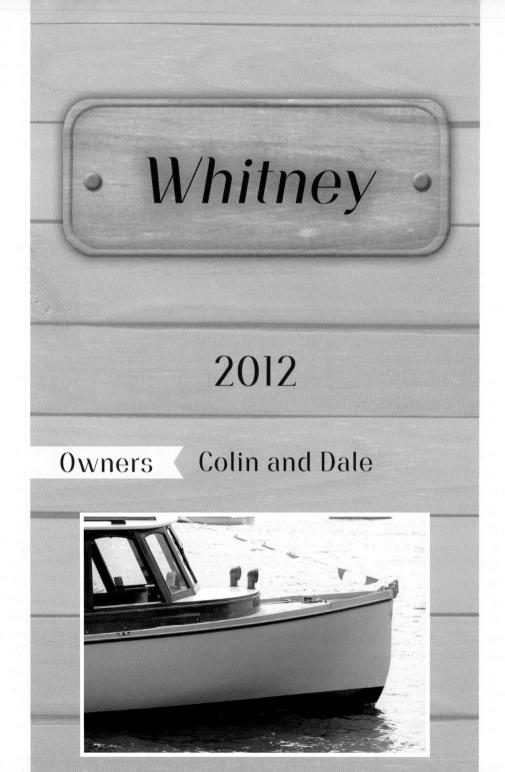

Whitney was designed by Bruce Askew from photos of boats that Colin had taken. He had a fair idea of what he wanted — a traditional-looking lake boat with lots of cabin and cockpit seating room. Bruce crafted Colin's ideas into the design, managing to put the motor right at the front so as to allow for a spacious cabin. The overall length is 28 feet (8.5 m).

When Colin and Dale hit the 'go' button, the construction of the boat was handed over to Te Puna boat builder Mike Muir. Mike spent a year of his life building the boat and fell in love with the lines of her. Over the years, Mike had built a number of Bruce Askew-designed boats and has always enjoyed the work. The hull is constructed of edge-glued cedar and is glassed both sides. The deck and cockpit floor are glassed plywood, overlaid with teak. The cabin sides are solid teak with the cabin top made of cedar frames and plywood on both sides. Mike has made a stunning job of *Whitney* and, unless you were advised otherwise, you would think you were looking at an immaculate restoration of a turn-of-the-20th-century launch.

Colin and Dale absolutely love their new boat and really enjoy cruising in her and fishing off her.

Richmond Rose

1908

Owner Wayne ('Brownie')

Spotted on the Whitianga waterways, this pretty little craft had spent previous time on inland lakes and in Tauranga.

For the past 25 years owner Wayne ('Brownie') has looked after this beautiful 26-foot (7.9 m) Logan launch. It was thought to have been built in 1908, according to the highly respected old-time boat builders Brownie talked to some 25 years ago. Some of the clues were in the rounded cabin front and the solid kauri Samson post.

She was derelict in a farmer's paddock in Orini (Waikato) when Brownie found her in 1990. The subsequent purchase was followed by a massive restoration effort by Brownie. All the ribs were replaced, the cabin was removed and shortened to create more cockpit space, and the hull was re-caulked. It took three years for the restoration, and the boat was baptised *Richmond Rose* after Brownie's children, the original name having long since disappeared. Brownie's research to date has not brought the original name to light.

Brownie re-powered the shoal draught launch with a high-thrust four-stroke 9.9 hp Yamaha outboard, housed in a covered inboard-outboard well near the transom. This immediately freed up cabin space by not having to house a hulking great motor and box in the cabin. The hidden outboard drives the boat comfortably at a hull speed of 9 knots, and it is very quiet and incredibly economical to run.

Some years later, Brownie gave the hull a revamp. Using late-20th-century technology, the hull was splined and glassed. The gaps between the planking were stripped of their caulking and filled with an epoxy resin. The hull was then glassed in 10 oz cloth, faired and painted in two-pot Altex paint. The hull is now watertight, stronger and ready for another 100 years of use.

The boat has attractive upholstery in the cockpit and the cabin. It is well endowed with brass work, and has some lovely carved panels. All in all, *Richmond Rose* is a lovely old boat that captures those stunning Logan lines beautifully.

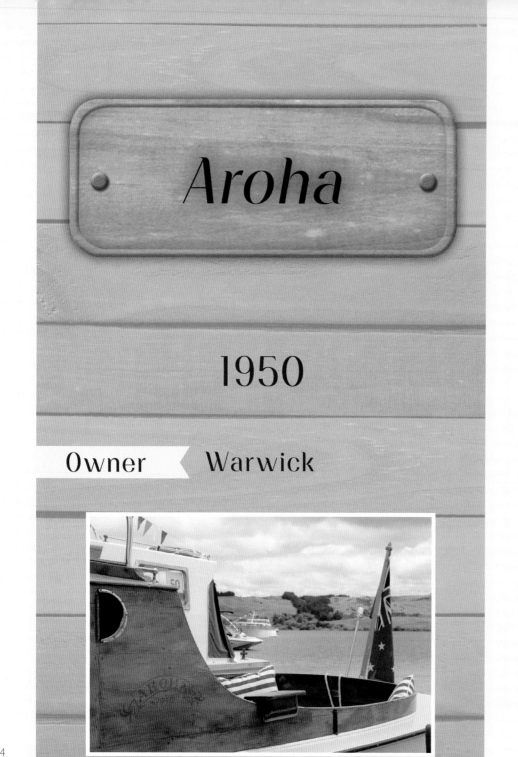

Aroha

1950

This 21-foot (6.4 m) carvel-planked, kauri-hulled launch was designed and built by CE Thompson in Dargaville. She was fitted with a Scottish Kelvin Ricardo four-cylinder side-valve petrol (or paraffin) engine, featuring two sets of two cylinders, with separate carburettors on each, enabling either pair to be individually switched off and allowing the boat to motor on just two cylinders. The motor was designed by Anton Bergius of Glasgow, with many of them fitted in Scottish trawlers.

Aroha was hauled by road from Dargaville and launched at Mourea (between lakes Rotorua and Rotoiti) in 1950. The launch has spent her entire life on Lake Rotoiti at Otaramarae Bay, housed in a boatshed. She still has her original colours, accessories, paintwork, trim, tools, striped canvas cushions and manuals. She even carries the original boat hook, oar, anchor and warp, and spotlight.

The current owner was lucky enough to find this little honey in 2002. She had never really had a name, as the Macklow family, who owned the boat from new through to 2002, called her 'the launch' or 'Mako'— an abbreviation of the family name.

Warwick renamed her *Aroha* ('love') after his mother. His mum had purchased a bach at Otaramarae Bay in 1950 so perhaps he'd had the inside running in buying this wee gem of a boat. An official naming ceremony was held in October 2002 at Otaramarae Bay. The boat was blessed by Henry Morehu of Ngati Pikiao.

Ellen

2005 (1900 plan)

Owners Grant and Helen

I was very taken with this little launch and was having a hard time trying to put a date on her. I put it very early in the 1900s yet I could not get over the condition of her. She really was amazing. In fact, she looked darn near like a new boat. To my great surprise, I found that she had been built and launched in 2005. This piqued my interest even more because I realised she had been copied off a very old design. Fortunately, I was able to get more information on this lovely craft from the owners Helen and Grant so, in their own words, here is the story behind the beautiful *Ellen*:

Ellen is a 'Waihou 8' turn-of-the-century replica of a New Zealand settlers' river launch. She has a 2.2 m beam, draws 0.6 m, and is 8 m in overall length. Built in strip-plank cedar, using an old hull found behind Tom Hunt's boatshed at Kopu (Thames) as a plug, she is a classic proven displacement hull, blended with modern wooden boat-building technology by Malcolm Sowman, the boat builder. The boat has a tandem-axle trailer and is easily towed.

The original hull from which Ellen *was built has only one distinguishing feature and that is the number '573' stencilled on the bow. The story goes that this hull started life in Northland, probably as a yacht. She eventually ended up being used as transport on the Waihou River and is probably more than 115 years old. Malcolm Sowman acquired the old hull as settlement of a debt and teamed up with Tom Hunt to build the new boat using the old one as a pattern.*

She was purchased by us in February 2006 as a result of Tom taking the boat to the Lake Rotoiti Wooden Boat Association Parade that year and putting a 'For Sale' sign on her. We commissioned Malcolm to add the cabin top and front windscreen. A Nanni 29 hp three-cylinder diesel was fitted, and an Eberspächer diesel heater. All trim work was done by Bill Beskett at Kopu and has been kept very traditional. A hideaway Navman Trackfish 650 was also fitted.

In November 2006, *Ellen* was officially launched in her new form by Helen and Grant at a 'double launch', with Allan and Ronda Clark's new wooden boat *Princess* (see page 238).

Ellen is one of those boats that just catches your eye, even if you don't have a particular interest in boats.

Elva

1911

Owner Grant

Elva was built by Collings and Bell and was displayed at the 1912 Auckland Boat Show. Her name is a tribute to one of Mr Collings' three daughters.

Owned by Hugh Preston, *Elva* was used around Auckland, Kawau and Great Barrier Islands.

The next known or remembered owner was Malcolm Pearce, who purchased her from an owner north of Auckland. One presumes she passed through a few sets of hands before Malcolm acquired her, but little is known of those intervening years. At that stage she needed a repaint and some regular maintenance.

In 2004, Grant and his friend Nigel Brock bought the boat, with Grant buying out Nigel's share at a later date.

Her overall length is 22 feet (6.7 m). She is designed as a day boat and with her great lines looks absolutely lovely on the water.

Phantom

Circa 1920s

Phantom is a 4.8 m carvel-planked settler's launch. She was found beached near Colville Bay in the Coromandel before World War Two and was considered an old boat even then. She was found by the late John Goudie, who had her repaired and powered with a Stuart Turner 4 hp motor in the mid-'50s. She stayed in Colville Bay until the late '90s when she was put into storage.

Mick purchased the boat in 2007. He stripped and re-caulked the hull, replaced the transom-mounted rudder, and made some small seating alterations.

The engine was replaced with a Yanmar of 1970s vintage, and the boat has had many good seasons on the Rotorua and Waikato hydro lakes ever since.

The Mullet Boat

The mullet boat, often called a 'mullety', was originally designed and developed in 1870s New Zealand as a fishing boat. Its main use was for netting mullet in the shallow estuaries near Thames.

The mullet boats were generally about 24 feet (7.3 m) in length, although this could vary. They had a centreboard that could be raised to allow for working in the shallows, then dropped to prevent lateral motion when under sail. This also meant that they could sail upwind quite well.

Mullet boats also had a broad transom for the crew of two to use a net over. They were rigged with a large set of sails so as to be able to sail quickly back to Auckland with their catch.

Over time, they became more refined and so became quicker. This sometimes led to skippers racing each other on return trips. Soon their popularity rose in the racing scene and it wasn't long before they became exclusively racing boats.

By 1900 they had become a pleasure boat rather than a working boat.

Up until World War Two, they were prominent in the Auckland yacht-racing fleet. However, along the way, a few of the mullet boats lost their sails and gained cabins, thus transforming them into launches or settler-style lake boats like the two boats featured: *Aratu* and *MV Snark*.

Aratu

1923

Owner   Ross

The name 'Aratu' in Maori means 'pathway to great heights'. *Aratu* was built from heart kauri in 1923, by Archie Logan. She has a mullet hull, measuring just 17 feet (5.2 m) with a 6 ft 6 in (2 m) beam, and she actually boasts two berths.

She was originally owned by a New Zealand-based Italian commercial fisherman, who still owned her at the outbreak of World War Two. Legend has it that, concerned about a possible invasion, he re-powered the boat so that it went faster in reverse than it did going forward!

When the fisherman retired, the boat was on-sold, and distinguished itself by being the boat that the owners at the time won the 1987 New Zealand Open Game Fishing Nationals in.

The boat is extremely seaworthy, having cruised to Mayor Island and all up and down the Bay of Plenty coastline.

Aratu has been re-powered with a two-cylinder diesel and cruises at 9 knots.

MV *Snark*

1912

Owners ▷ **William and Caroline**

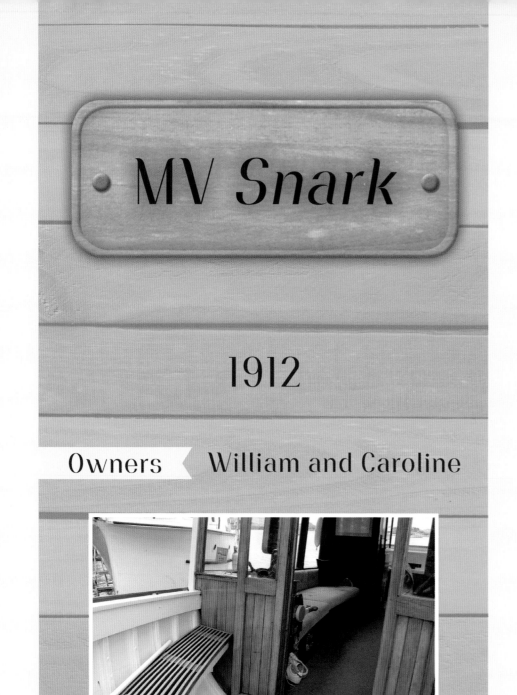

The motor vessel *Snark* is a mullet design, originally built in 1912. She measures 7.8 metres in length and originally would have been a sailboat running a gaff rig. At some stage in her life she was sailed down to Tauranga, where she was later abandoned.

Many years later, the abandoned hull was recovered from the mud in Tauranga harbour by Geoff Main.

MV *Snark* was rebuilt in 1990 and reconfigured on the topsides to a lake day boat style. The large day cabin can carry a number of people, and with the front of the cabin opening up to an outdoor bow seating area, offers extra versatility. At the stern you can see that an additional counter stern has been added to gain extra length. It is not until you look closely that the shaft of a small high-thrust outboard motor can be seen. The outboard is pretty well hidden and frees up all the internal space that otherwise would have to accommodate an internal motor. A very cunning move by Geoff.

Relaunched in 1992, she has plied the lake waters ever since, entertaining many people on the way. She has lovely lines that will always attract the eye. Little is known of her life and how many years she lay in the mud, but it is great to see her restored and being enjoyed again.

Classic Runabouts and Cabin Cruisers

In my boating career I have owned five boats that could be described as 'runabouts' or 'cabin cruisers'. They were mostly examples built in fibreglass and aluminium. However, the earlier types and styles of boats featured here were the forerunners to the fibreglass and aluminium runabouts and cabin boats of today. Built in timber, they were, with the odd exception, generally reasonably quick for their time and powered by either a marinised petrol car engine, or an outboard. Some were quite plain, others quite pretty, while a few special boats had lines that could only be described as stunningly beautiful.

As a small boy I was brought up with trailer boats designed by the likes of John Spencer, Carl Augustin, Richard Hartley, Frank Pelin and Tony Mason, first with his Marlins and, later, his Clippers. They were the designers of the day and their designs graced many a beach in the '50s and '60s. Even the Glen-L designs from the *Popular Mechanics* magazine were built by home builders in reasonable numbers. These types of boat were common among the boaties of the period and many families started off boating in them, including ours. I owned two wooden speedboats prior to purchasing my first runabout (a 1966 fibreglass CrestaCraft) in late 1975.

Over the years the restoration of old launches and yachts has been growing, but the smaller trailer boats have taken a lot longer to become valued collector boats. It is great to see a revival of interest in these craft because they are just as significant as the larger craft. They were a major part of the backbone of the New Zealand boating industry and boating scene in their day.

Summertime

2014 (1969 plan)

Owner/Builder — Rosie

Rosie is a remarkable young woman. A couple of years ago she attended a classic boat regatta with her parents and brother at St Arnaud. While there she saw a lovely little Pelin Venturer called *Full of Fun*. She fell in love with the look of the boat and decided then and there that she wanted one. The only problem was she couldn't find one, but somebody acquired a set of plans and gave them to Rosie.

She decided to build one! She took some boat-building lessons from a retired boat builder and cut her teeth on a dinghy, which now hangs from the ceiling in her parents' garage. Over the following two years she built the Pelin, also in her parents' garage, complete with a beautiful varnished deck.

The quality of the build is absolutely stunning and would be a credit to any professional boat builder. The hull is carbon ply, imported from Israel for both its strength and lightness. The deck timber is teak with inlaid holly, and the windscreen is beautifully encased in teak timber. A white vinyl back-to-back bench seat sets off the interior. The floor is varnished over ply that incorporates macrocarpa sawdust to create a non-slip finish.

At a recent Antique and Classic Boat Show at St Arnaud, Rosie not only won a race for her class of boat, but also took out the top award. It just goes to prove that girls can do anything, including building a stunning boat by themselves. Rosie is just 26 years old.

Sparkle Horse

1955

This is a darling of a boat. Named the Palomino model, *Sparkle Horse* is a small 15-foot (4.6 m) Century outboard runabout, and is one of a range of pleasure boats built by this very successful American company. Phillip originally saw this boat in a museum in the States and fell in love with it. It is easy to see why. The boat was actually for sale, but the owner wanted US$30,000 for it, which was somewhat over the top. A year or two later, Phillip got a call from a friend in the States to say that the museum had gone broke and all the boats were going up for auction. He wired his friend NZ$15,000 with a request to buy the little Century if he could. His friend bid on the boat and got it for NZ$14,000. Phillip was delighted and the boat subsequently arrived in New Zealand.

The boat is powered by an original 50 hp Johnson outboard motor, manufactured in 1957. It has a huge casing (for a 50 hp motor) and it makes you realise just how much outboard technology has progressed over the years, with outboards getting more compact and more powerful. The whole rig is very appealing and the boat still carries its original and unique calfskin vinyl seats. It is believed to be one of only two Century Palominos in the world to still carry the original seat coverings.

The boat did not have a name when it arrived in New Zealand, so the name *Sparkle Horse* was thought up by Phillip's kids and seemed somehow appropriate for a boat with the model name 'Palomino'.

Marlin/ Marauder

Circa 1959

Colin inherited this boat from his dad, who had bought it in the mid-'70s. I have always had a soft spot for the Marlin, ever since two of my dad's friends bought them. They were both 17-footers (5.2 m) and had the same lower cabin configuration as this boat. In fact, these boats brought about my first case of boat envy!

The Marauder was always the 19-foot (5.8 m) version, and had the additional hardtop. This boat was originally powered by a six-cylinder Greys marine petrol engine and developed around 100 hp. At a later date the boat was fitted with a 50 hp Yanmar turbo diesel, which it still has today. Colin reports that the boat still gets up and planes comfortably with the diesel. He said it is quite a heavy boat, but handles a good-sized chop with ease.

The Marlin was designed by Tony Mason and built by Sutton Mason Marine. Tony later went on to form Mason Marine and designed and built the stunning Clipper range of cabin cruisers, ranging from 20 to 26 feet (6.1 to 7.9 m). The Clipper, in my humble opinion, was the finest cabin boat produced at the time in New Zealand. Its predecessor, the Marlin, though generally smaller, was a very close second and, of course, designed by the same person. These are a very pretty boat with great lines. My dad and I always had an ability to look at a boat and just know whether the designer had got it right or not. This probably came from all our years designing our Liteweight caravans. To me, the Marlin came close, and is still near perfection in its lines and eye appeal.

These boats were great performers in their day and will become very sought after as the restoration of cabin boats and speedboats gathers momentum, just as the launches before them, and historic yachts before them.

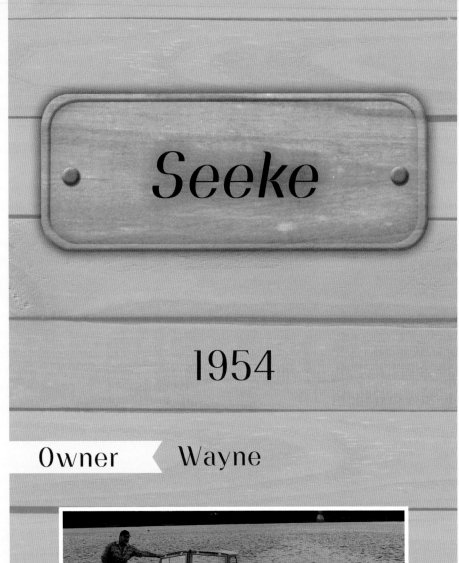

Seeke

1954

Seeke was built for Wayne's granddad, Ernie Pask. This is an excellent example of the very popular range of home-built boats typical of the 1950s. Many of these smaller boats, such as this 12-footer (3.7 m), were amateur-built from professional plans, making the boat affordable to an average family.

Seeke was built in mahogany ply with Oregon stringers, and varnished throughout. At that stage she sported a small cabin. Ernie decided he would call the boat 'Seeker', simply because *Sea Spray* magazine was giving away some new-fangled stick-on letters. Ernie carefully stuck on the letters, but made a mistake sticking on the last letter — 'R' — so the boat became *Seeke*, pronounced 'See- key'.

At some point in time, Granddad Ernie decided to paint the hull. As the years went by he painted the hull many times. After he died, one of the sons got the boat. It was seldom used and had been sitting in a shed for many years. About 25 years ago, Wayne acquired the boat from his uncle and set about restoring it. He removed the cabin top, leaving the cabin front and sides, which made a lovely windscreen. Along the way, he discovered under the layers of paint that the boat had originally been varnished. So began the tedious job of stripping off the paint, then re-varnishing. The transom was badly marked so Wayne overlaid mahogany ply, then fibreglassed the bottom of the boat. The outboard had always clamped onto the transom, so Wayne built in a well. He fitted a 1970 18 hp Evinrude engine. When it gave up the ghost, Wayne bought a 1965 18 hp Johnson for $100. It still powers the boat today.

Seeke II

2012 (1940s replica)

Owner Wayne

This boat is a revelation. It looks like an old boat, but it's not. Wayne designed and built this boat part-time in his garage. It was started in 2009 and launched in 2012. Wayne wanted a craft that looked as if it had been built in the 1940s. He wanted a lapstrake hull and a high sweeping bow, like the boats from the Orkney Islands in Scotland. Lapstrake hulls have a similar construction to clinker boats, only the wooden panels are wider. The hull is made of red Meranti plywood, which is known for its durability, lightness and stunning woodgrain. The frames are built from western red cedar, also known for its strength and lightness.

The boat has some lovely features, with rounded ply from the cabin sides blending into the cabin top. The front cabin windows open like VW Kombi vans' front 'splitty' windows. The boat also has a light hardtop that detaches very easily from the cabin top and stows neatly in the cockpit. This was so Wayne could get the boat into his shed.

Seeke II has quite a high-sided hull with a very shallow 'V' at the transom. It handles a good-sized chop with ease, and is a very dry boat. The varnished seats are both fitted with a fore and aft movable backrest. The boat is completely varnished and has instant appeal to most boaties and 'Joe and Joanne Public'. Wayne says she always gets a lot of attention wherever he goes with her. The boat is powered by an 18 hp four-stroke Tohatsu outboard and performs very well. The motor was a few years old but had only 30 minutes' running logged when Wayne bought her.

Wayne also collects old boat magazines and plans, and has a stunning collection of 1950s and '60s *Sea Spray* magazines. He even has a 1949 issue. As a kid I couldn't wait for the latest boat magazines to come out so I was delighted to have a chance to pore over his collection. He also has catalogues of boat plans by Carl Augustin and John Spencer from the '50s and '60s. How valuable would they be?

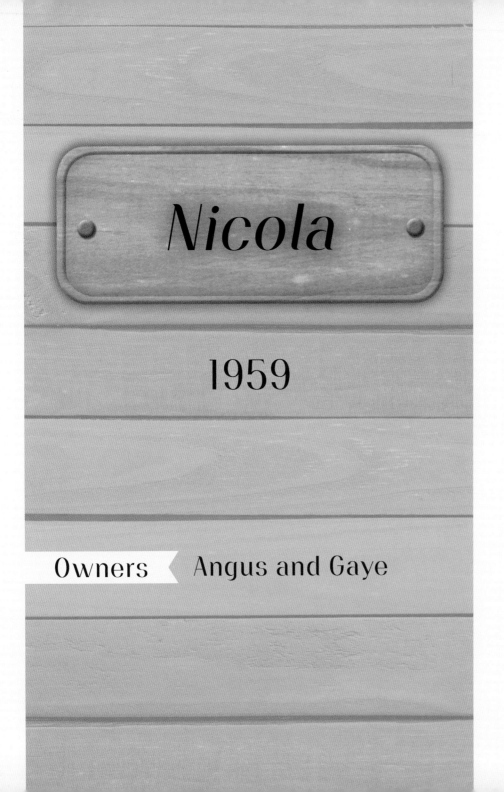

Nicola

1959

Owners   Angus and Gaye

Nicola, like *Seeke*, is a very typical type of runabout that used to frequent New Zealand beaches, lakes and rivers in the late '50s and early '60s. She was built in 1959 and was for much of her life a 'Southern belle'. She was built in Dunedin by Patel & Sons Boat Builders for the proprietor of a sports shop. She boated on Lake Wakatipu until purchased by a Dr Insull in 1963. After that she was used mainly on Lake Te Anau, but also on lakes Manapouri and Wanaka. Originally powered by a Johnson outboard, she was upgraded with a 65 hp Mercury in 1974. The Insull family owned and enjoyed this boat for nearly 40 years.

She was gifted to the current owners in 2001. From 2004 to 2005 the hull and deck were restored to original condition. Both were sanded back to bare timber, the hull was repainted and the deck varnished. The windows were replaced, a new transom built, and the interior upholstery replaced to replicate how it was when it was purchased. She is 4.9 metres in length. Angus and Gaye plan to do further improvements to the interior in the future, but right now they are content to just sit back and enjoy having her in the water.

Ywoodenu

Circa late 1960s–early '70s

Owner Tim

This lovely-looking Pelin cabin cruiser was bought by the current owner in Christchurch in early 2013 after he spied it on Trade Me. A wooden trailer boat enthusiast, Tim could not resist adding it to his collection. Frank Pelin was a renowned boat designer producing many runabout, cabin boat and launch designs. According to the Pelin website, there are over 160 boat plans available, ranging from dinghies to runabouts, yachts, cabin cruisers and launches. Pelin's plans were geared for family boating and the amateur backyard boat builder, and naturally appealed to those with a quintessential 'Kiwi can-do' attitude.

Originally, the boat was home-built by a joiner/French polisher in Auckland, probably in the early '70s. It was only used a few times before the owner passed away. His widow kept the boat in her garage for many years until a family friend purchased it, then on-sold it to the Christchurch owner. When he gained possession of the boat, the motive power was a 40 hp Evinrude outboard. The Christchurch owner upgraded the outboard to a 90 hp Johnson, which is still on the boat. The Pelin itself is in original condition and features polished and varnished topsides in mahogany.

The boat was not named when Tim bought her, so the name *Ywoodenu* is quite appropriate. He lives in Taupo so the boat sees quite a bit of lake time.

Tim is a wooden boat enthusiast and owns four boats, including another Pelin, a Glen-L Swift, and a 1953 7-metre speedboat, which is still under restoration. It will be interesting to see what Tim's next project is.

Old Outboards

While researching this book, I came across many old outboards from the 1950s and '60s, a time in New Zealand when this type of marine motive power was just starting to become popular with boaties.

The following few pages of photographs portray a little of what I saw. Some of the outboards have some history of interest, but there are many about which little is known. Without exception, these old outboards are now incredibly rare, particularly if they are in running order, so enjoy what you see here.

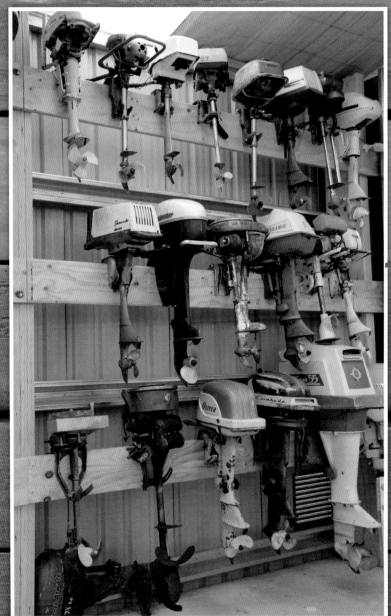

An early 1960s American Gale.

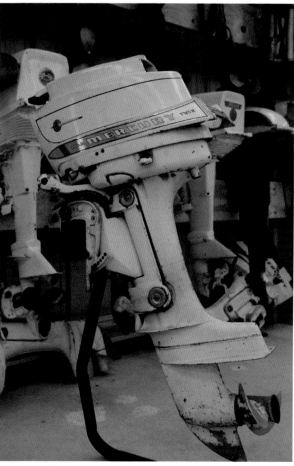

A late 1950s Mercury 10 hp.

A 1950 British Seagull 4 hp.

A 1950s Johnson 10 hp.

A mid-1950s Scott-Atwater 7.5 hp.

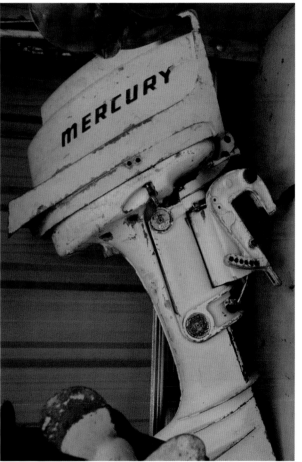

A 1959 Mercury 15 hp.

A 1957 Johnson 50 hp.

A 1955 Scott-Atwater 10 hp.

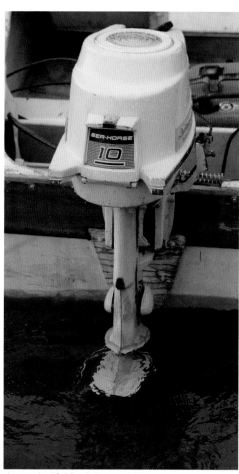

An early 1960s Johnson 10 hp.

A mid-1950s Scott-Atwater 33 hp.

An old outboard display.

The label says it all!

In Search of Speed

Some New Zealanders (and I would include myself in this category) have a need for speed and, in many cases, competition. Such individuals are often seen around car racing and motorcycle racing, and the same is true for boating. Speed lovers used to often take to yachting, but the advent of the powered boat provided an opportunity to hone that competitive edge. The famous Rudder Cup, a launch race on the Waitemata Harbour, took place over many years. As the smaller boats developed, we saw the appearance of the famous American speedboats and the 'gentleman racers' of the 1920s and '30s.

The popularity of speedboats in New Zealand and the ensuing racing really gained momentum after World War Two through the late 1940s, '50s and '60s, when more specialised boats began to dominate the boat-racing scene.

I can remember as a lad in the 1950s watching these speedboats race on the Waikato River, and my wife (a few years younger than me) can remember family picnics at the speedboat racing at Lake Karapiro in the 1960s.

As waterskiing developed as a popular sport, boats required more speed and torque to pull a skier out of the water, as they created a huge drag until they were up. This was even more evident when towing multiple skiers. This situation forced a move away from the true twin-cockpit boats to boats with a larger rear cockpit with a central motor cover and space to the sides, giving room to stow waterskis.

This section showcases some fine examples of old and replica ski boats, speedboats and racing boats, including the second boat I ever owned, *Canta Libre*. I enjoyed a rather emotional reunion with the boat some 32 years after owning her. I was thrilled to see she was still being cared for and in relatively good condition, given the many years since we enjoyed Sunday waterskiing each summer. Eight years after that and I was able to track her down again to feature in this book.

Canta Libre

Circa early 1950s

Owners Nelson and Judith

This vintage boat holds a special place in my heart, as back in 1973 to '75 I owned her.

I'd already had a smaller speedboat named *Sea Witch*, later named *Jezebel*, which was built in 1955 and powered by a 1500 cc GT Cortina motor. She was just 13 feet (4 m) long. My new acquisition, *Canta Libre*, measured 17 feet (5.2 m) in length and was powered by a small-block Chevrolet motor, sporting Corvette tappet covers. She was fairly tired-looking, with the hull painted a faded iridescent light blue. The deck was covered in what had once been a woodgrain vinyl, but was then a peeling, faded brown colour. It had twin cockpits, and a strong tumblehome with a narrow, sloped stern. The front seat was actually the back seat out of a Hillman Hunter. The back cockpit was pretty basic with a worn paint finish inside.

Despite the tired appearance, the boat was actually very sound, and the hull had been fibreglassed. I fell in love with her classical lines. The boat dealer told me she was designed and built by Carl Augustin, with the build era somewhere between the late 1940s to mid-'50s.

Once I got her, I ran her into the paint shop and gave the hull a coat of maroon enamel. I then filled in the front hatch and re-covered the deck in a cream vinyl. I used her like this for a year, during which time the motor gave up the ghost. I pulled it out, reconditioned it, and went on using her. Together with my flatmate John and my cousin Neil we used her mainly for waterskiing at Horahora, Karapiro and Taupo lakes.

In 1974, I started taking out a new girlfriend, Marilyn (who has been my wife for many years now). The old V8 speedboat was her first introduction to boats and, after taking her for a blat around the lake, she got a 15-minute instruction on how to drive it, then became our resident skipper while we all hung off the back on waterskis. Gary, her younger brother, soon joined the regular crew.

Marilyn and Don in Canta Libre.

About to pull four skiers out. From left: Neil Jessen, Roy Paterson, Don Jessen, Dave McRobbie. Boat driver is Terry Stevenson, and lookout, Marilyn Jessen.

Maybe this is why I have such a soft spot for *Canta Libre*.

I decided to redo the interior. The Hillman Hunter seat was biffed and Marilyn and I fitted buttoned black vinyl upholstery to the front cockpit. The back cockpit got the full treatment, with the engine box, the floor, sides and back all fitted with two-inch (5 cm) foam, and again covered in buttoned black vinyl upholstery.

We wanted a name for her and our favourite song at the time was Neil Diamond's 'Canta Libre', so *Canta Libre* she became, with the name proudly sign-written across her stern. It translates as 'Sing free'. She was capable of popping four adults out of the water in single-ski deep-water starts. We would generally arrive out at the lake at 7.30 a.m. and ski until it got dark, pulling the boat out around lunchtime to do a quick trip to the gas station to refill her, and dropping her back in to carry on for the rest of the day.

This routine would usually start the weekend after Labour Day (spent on Lake Taupo), and run through every Sunday to Christmas, then back to Taupo for the holidays, then back into it till Easter, then another trip to Taupo at Easter to

finish the season. In my younger days I skied right across Lake Taupo and back again behind *Canta Libre*. I couldn't do that now. Even thinking about it makes me tired!

In late 1975 I traded her on a 1966 fibreglass 14-foot (4.3 m) CrestaCraft, fitted with a Johnson Stinger racing outboard. I heard that *Canta Libre* had been sold to a guy in Rotorua, then I completely lost track of her.

Many years later (around 2007, I think), I was idly cruising the net and came across the Lake Rotoiti Wooden Boat Parade and, lo and behold, there she was! I got hold of the owners and suggested to them that their boat might have once been owned by me. They invited Marilyn and me across to their home at the Mount and, sure enough, it was our old *Canta Libre*. Just to add to the coincidences, the owners both had connections to my wife. It turned out that Judith had gone to high school with Marilyn, and her husband, Nelson, was the nephew of Marilyn's mum's best friend. Talk about a small world! As you tend to do, we lost contact with Nelson and Judith so it was with great delight that I managed to track them down again to feature the boat in the book.

The following is Judith and Nelson's story of their journey with *Canta Libre*: Judith had gone to the Rotorua dump to drop off some rubbish and was having a look around to see if any 'treasure' had turned up. She fell into conversation with a woman who told her about an old wooden boat she had sitting in her paddock. She asked if Judith's husband would be interested in it. The boat's motor had broken down and it had been out of the water since 1981. Apparently, the woman's husband had died halfway through repairing it.

Judith debated mentioning it to Nelson for a day or two. But together, they ended up investigating the boat, with Nelson becoming quickly excited when he realised it was a twin-cockpit speedboat complete with barrelback, tumblehome and sloped transom. There was an old V8 with Corvette rocker covers sitting on planks across it. The boat had deteriorated sitting out in the paddock, and there was a hole in the side and the deck looked pretty suspect. The trailer, however, which appeared to be specifically built for the boat, was in good condition.

Nelson and Judith swapped a garden trailer for the whole rig and carted it home to the Mount. The restoration took a year (part-time) of Nelson's time. The hull was repaired and painted, again in maroon with the boat's name faithfully rewritten on the stern, copying the faint outline of the previous signwriting. A completely new teak and holly deck was laid, and the old windscreen was replaced with a period 1930s-style glass screen. The old 283 ci Chevrolet motor was ruined so it was replaced with a more powerful 302 ci Chev. A burr elm dashboard, as seen in Jaguar car models, was fitted, along with a mahogany Momo steering wheel and new retro gauges, as the original speedo was broken. The final touch was to fit leopard skin-covered seats.

Nelson and Judith have owned *Canta Libre* for some years now, and swear they will never part with her. Knowing our history with the boat, and the fact that *Canta Libre* played a part in Nelson and Judith's own daughter's romance, they jokingly call her 'the love boat'!

With the new motor *Canta Libre* is somewhat faster than she used to be, reaching an incredible 50 mph. In our day, with the smaller V8, she could only manage 40 mph but, man, could she pull multiple skiers! Nelson tells me she still has the same prop so she no doubt still has the same pulling power.

Rumrunner

1970

Owner — Leith

As young lads in the 1960s, Leith and his older brother John used to hang around Leo Young's boat-building business that was close to their parents' home in Auckland. At the ages of 20 and 21, the brothers bought the plans for a Draco 5.4-metre speedboat that Young had designed, along with a Young marinised Ford Falcon motor and fittings. Under the mentorship of Leo Young, the two brothers built their speedboat in their parents' garage in 12 months, and proudly named her *Rumrunner*, with a nod to the prohibition era in America. It was 1970, and *Rumrunner* was built with kahikatea frames and stringers, and a plywood hull. The boys used the boat regularly on the Auckland Harbour and the Rotorua lakes. They even once took the boat from Half Moon Bay to Russell, in the Bay of Islands, completing the voyage without any dramas.

By 1984 the brothers were using the boat less and less so the decision was made to sell her. She was sold to John Snow of Weymouth, who ran her for many years on the Manukau Harbour, often taking her across the bar. In 2005, though, John decided to sell *Rumrunner* and offered her back to Leith.

Leith couldn't resist the temptation to own the boat he and his brother had built all those years ago. It was a bit tired after all the years of use so Leith and his good friend Murray Binning began a full restoration. They replaced the deck with mahogany plywood, which was sprayed with 10 coats of varnish. The hull received a repaint, and a new instrument panel went in with everything you could possibly wish for. The original Falcon 3.6 was replaced with a later-model 4.1 litre, and all the chrome fittings were re-chromed. Sadly, Murray passed away in 2008 after a courageous battle against leukaemia before he was able to enjoy a trip out in *Rumrunner*.

Later in 2008, Leith came across a fully restored Falcon Bathurst 4.1-litre motor of 1974 vintage. It developed 200 hp and Leith couldn't resist buying it and fitting it in *Rumrunner*. The engine, like in many speedboats of the era, is raw water-cooled with exhausts exiting through the transom. Under way she sounds awesome. There is no reverse gear, but Leith has fitted a clutch so he has a neutral. This again was fairly typical of the average speedboat of the time. The hull is fairly flat at the stern and is a little hard-riding, but she has plenty of lowdown grunt and is great for single-ski deep-water starts. She has a sweet cruising spot of around 25 knots.

Leith uses the boat on the Auckland Harbour, Lake Karapiro and the Rotorua lakes. He says the boat is a bit of an obsession. Looking at the lines of the boat and, of course, its history, I can understand his obsession completely. There are believed to be about four 'Dracos' left in the country, so *Rumrunner* has become a very rare boat indeed.

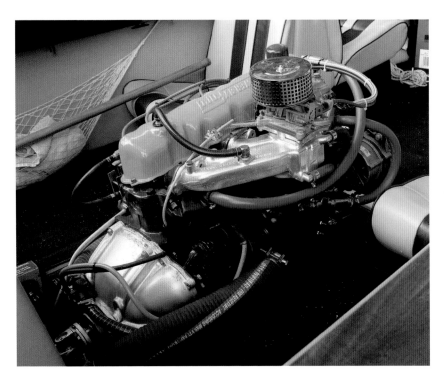

Seconda Mano

1957

Owner Unknown

I didn't have a lot of time to talk to the owners of this early original ski boat but I did manage to get a very brief history of their involvement with her.

The owners spotted her during a holiday in Europe. They were so taken with her beautiful classical lines that they bought her and had her shipped back to New Zealand. It is an Italian-built Riva, the design of which is said to have been inspired by the American company, Chris-Craft.

The Riva Boat Company was founded by Pietro Riva and was family-run from 1842 to 1969, and, after being sold, continued to produce boats up until 1996. The Riva's speed, beauty and craftsmanship earned it the reputation of the 'Ferrari of the boating world'. Its hull is varnished mahogany and it is just beautiful. The classic lines are stunningly sculptured so that the boat looks fast even when anchored. The designer got it just right. This boat was bought second-hand and, translated, is exactly what the exotic-sounding name 'Seconda Mano' means.

Under power she looks beautiful, with a curl of spray trailing back from her stern, instantly bringing back fond memories to me of my old *Canta Libre* days (see page 114).

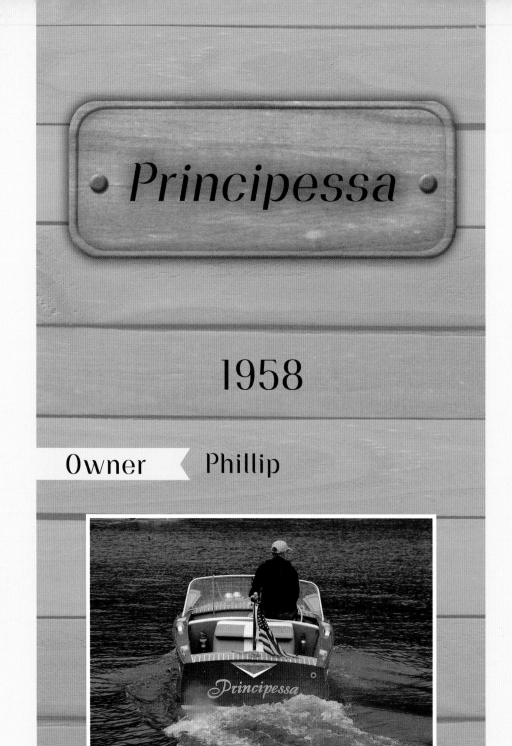

Principipessa

1958

Owner Phillip

Principipessa is a 16-foot (4.9 m) Resorter, made by Century Boats in the US. It was a very popular boat in its heyday. Originally formed in 1926 by two brothers in Milwaukee, Wisconsin, Century Boats moved to Michigan in 1928, and produced a range of performance, fishing and pleasure boats. During World War Two, Century produced patrol boats, then returned to pleasure boats again after the war. The Resorter model was first built in the early 1950s. With the larger cockpit in the rear and a small covered motor box, people could move around the boat a little easier, and when waterskiing became popular the boat was ideally suited, compared with the full twin-cockpit models. The Resorter was chosen as the official boat for the US national and international ski competitions throughout the latter half of the '50s.

Principipessa's construction is from mahogany and avodire timber, an African white mahogany. The upholstery is original and the hull has been re-varnished. The boat is powered by a Ford Interceptor V8, creating 150 hp, and is the original motor. Phillip found the boat in Portland, Oregon, and imported it in 2007.

The trailer was pretty suspect so Phillip had an aluminium one built to a retro-styled plan. After the build it was painted in a light fawn/brown colour and the name 'Principipessa' was signwritten on both sides of the trailer. To set it off, Phillip used chrome wheels with whitewall tyres. On the trailer the boat looks period-perfect, and on the water she looks just as good. I was really taken with her, and was also very interested in the engineering and style of the trailer. Phillip has obviously put a lot of thought into the retro-looking trailer, and the attention to detail has, in my opinion, really paid off. In or out of the water the rig looks just perfect.

Some readers may have noticed that Phillip owns another Century boat (*Sparkle Horse*, see page 94). Read on, as he actually owns three (see the third, *Miss Tahoe*, on page 170). What a lucky man!

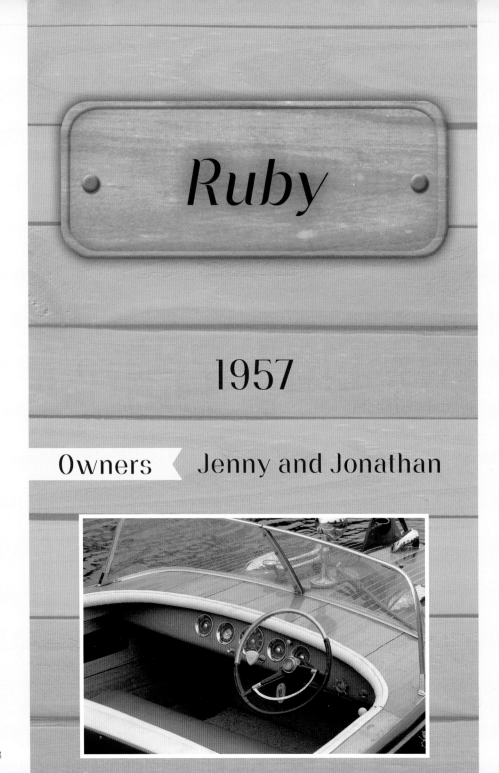

Ruby

1957

Owners Jenny and Jonathan

Chris-Craft is a well-known American brand of boat that, believe it or not, dates back as far as 1874. During the 1920s, '30s, '40s and '50s they were rather famous in the States for their varnished mahogany speedboats and runabouts. They came in all shapes and sizes, but the Chris-Craft pedigree was evident in each boat.

These boats were rarely seen in New Zealand during the high period of production, but I remember, as a lad, reading Dad's American boat magazines and being absolutely fascinated with the highly varnished boats of the time. The names Chris-Craft, Century Boats and Hacker-Craft were indelibly imprinted on my mind. To see these beautiful boats now appearing in New Zealand gladdens my heart.

Ruby is a 1957 Chris-Craft Continental model. She is a fully original mahogany speedboat and is powered by a Gray Marine V8 283 ci, which is, in fact, a professionally marinised Rambler Rebel V8 car motor.

Ruby was imported into New Zealand in 2004, where she spent time in Queenstown before getting her bottom professionally glassed by a boat builder in Invercargill.

Jenny and Jonathan subsequently purchased her and brought her back to Auckland to use there and on Lake Taupo.

Ruby was given a full engine rebuild in 2013, before attending a classic boat regatta on Lake Rotoiti, St Arnaud, in the Nelson Lakes area. Jenny and Jonathan so loved the place that they arranged to store the boat in the Nelson Lakes Classic Boat Museum and fly down from Auckland every three months for weekends on the water.

Judy H

2005 (1950s replica)

Owners Shawn and Cathy

I first saw *Judy H* when she pulled in beside my 1956 Packard and 1956 Liteweight Kiwi caravan combination at the 2011 Beach Hop. I was greatly taken with her, especially as I had owned two twin-cockpit ski boats in the early '70s.

The next time I saw her was at a Rotorua lake in 2014. Owners Shawn and Cathy hail from Taupo and their boat was a sure candidate for this book as a great example of a 'fast lady'.

In Cathy's words, here is the story of *Judy H*:

It was summer of 2002 and my soon-to-be-husband was enjoying a fascinating tour of my Uncle Bruce's shed at his Hawke's Bay orchard.

Uncle Bruce, an enthusiast and collector of all things automotive, had picked up this once lake-worthy 19 ft 6 in [5.9 m] replica of what most closely resembles an early Dodge watercraft. She sat in a very tired state on a period trailer under layers of similarly-aged candlewick bedspreads. After much admiration of all my uncle's trinkets, Shawn finally plucked up the courage to ask what was hidden beneath the blankets. These were thrown back, revealing the unmistakable classic lines of this once-loved powerboat.

Looking back on this day suggests that Shawn could see only gleaming polished mahogany deck hardware, and was completely oblivious to the task ahead. Over the coming months reality set in and the team at Dale Boat Builders was called in to evaluate the job. Company owner Bernie Dale's answer: 'It's the same price to build a new replica as it is to fix this.'

Bernie's father accepted the challenge of a complete rebuild, recycling only a few bits of timber and a re-chromed bollard from the old vessel. It was a fantastic 'journey', with many trips to the Dales' boatyard. Our involvement in some of the many decisions to be made really made us feel involved in the project: such things as windscreen shape and rake, engine and instrument choice to the finer points of varnish and upholstery, not to mention the lavish deck hardware we imported from the States.

On completion of Judy H, just prior to Christmas 2005, we planned a trip to take her back to Hastings for what was to be an epic surprise for my Uncle Bruce, who had inspired this dream. For good reason we had kept Bruce in the dark as to the progress we had been making on the boat over a nearly two-year period.

On Christmas Eve, on a gorgeous morning trip to the Bay, we borrowed a 1960 Dodge to tow our beauty with. On arrival, some of the most wonderful memories were made as we watched Bruce's eyes fog in a mist of pure enjoyment. This boat was real.

To date, our family has enjoyed many days on Lake Taupo and, most fondly, at seven of Lake Rotoiti's Classic and Wooden Boat Parades, a not-to-be-missed event on each year's calendar.

Judy H, a mahogany over ply runabout named after my late mother, Judy Hammond (Uncle Bruce's sister), is powered by a 350 ci fuel-injected V8.

Bootlegger

2005 (1940s replica)

The term 'barrelback' was used to describe a particular style of speedboat that was popular in the late 1930s and '40s. A lot of these boats were built in America by companies such as Chris-Craft, Century Boats and Hacker-Craft. They were easily recognised by the distinctive half barrel-shaped transom and the rolled sides, known by the term 'tumblehome'. The barrelbacks were phased out in the mid to late-'40s, although the tumblehome feature of the sides continued for a number of years.

Bootlegger was designed by Ken Hankinson and built by owner Greg. She took an estimated 2500 hours to complete and was launched in 2005.

Her overall length is 19 ft 6 in (5.9 m). The hull has kauri frames with a skin of cold-moulded ply (cold-moulding is the process of laminating layers of strips of ply at diagonals; this allows for compounding shapes to be built into the hull). The hull bottom has four layers of ply and is half an inch (1.3 cm) thick. The hull sides have two layers of ply, and are finished in mahogany. The deck covering boards (around the sides) are walnut, with the inside of the deck finished in mahogany and kauri stripes. The dash is mahogany with a rewarewa timber insert.

The motive power is a marinised 350 ci Chevrolet engine with a 1:1 marine gearbox — straight drive — connected to a 12 x 15-inch (30 x 38 cm) three-blade propeller. Other features include a traditionally built brass/chrome cutwater (bow cap), flush-look hardware, including pop-up navigation lights, and replica Chris-Craft windscreen frames. *Bootlegger* has a top speed of 45 mph.

There is no doubt that this boat has been a labour of love and Greg has made a fantastic job of her, and as if building *Bootlegger* was not enough, Greg then built a Glen-L-designed Squirt speedboat for the kids. It's a little beauty and is named *Gangsta*.

Both boats look brilliant out on the water and bring back nostalgic memories. Imagine what it must have been like owning boats like these two when they were brand new! Pretty awesome, I should think. Pretty awesome owning one today, too!

Misty

1998 (1930s replica)

Owner   Nigel

This boat is a replica styled on a 1930s gentleman's racer, and was made in New Zealand in 1998 by Classic Craft Boats in Auckland. The company made a number of boats in the 1990s and there are several 19-footers (5.8 m) similar to *Misty*.

She is based on a 1930 American Hacker-Craft runabout. Hacker-Craft boats, from Detroit, were very popular with their highly polished mahogany timber finishes and signature look. The founder of Hacker-Craft, John Hacker, is reputed to have been a good friend of Henry Ford and was instrumental in the growing popularity of planing boats.

Misty is powered by a 352 ci V8 motor. The construction comprises 6 mm sapele mahogany with maple insets over diagonal marine ply, laid over solid kauri frames and two large 90 x 90 mm engine bearers. Sapele mahogany is a medium-weight timber known for its high strength and beautiful woodgrain, as well as its rich red colour. *Misty*'s modern construction and design means the boat handles very well and is capable of doing 42 mph.

Nigel bought her in 2009 from Lake Rotoiti in the North Island, but she is now a regular at lakes Hawea and Wanaka in the south of the country. Once a year Nigel does the 11-hour drive up to the other Lake Rotoiti, in the Nelson Lakes district, to attend the Antique and Classic Boat Show and Regatta.

In 2014, Nigel sanded *Misty* back to bare wood and applied many coats of epoxy on the hull to show off the mahogany and maple woodwork. The hours of work this took have been well rewarded by the mirror-like finish on the decks.

This boat is not the only labour of love for Nigel, who also owns a 1950s triple-cockpit mahogany speedboat. He says these boats are quite addictive and somehow he managed to convince his very understanding wife that it would be safer if they had two wooden boats for picnics on the lakes.

Brave man! Or, perhaps, a very lucky man. Or just maybe his wife loves the romantic style of these boats as well? I can certainly understand that they could become addictive.

Nereid

1949 replica

Owners Les and Jeff

This is quite a story, not just of a boat but of a family. In 1949, the Johnson brothers, boat builders from Port Nelson, completed and launched a boat for Wesley Stilwell, a tobacco grower from Motueka. She was constructed in white pine plank and caulked. The hull cost the princely sum of £226. A 1934 Ford V8 motor was fitted, giving her a top speed of 32 mph. 'Nereid' means 'one from the sea', and, according to Greek mythology, sailors were assisted by the Nereids, daughters of the sea god.

Wesley raced his beloved *Nereid* from 1949 through to 1967 at Lake Rotoiti, Nelson Lakes, Lake Kaniere on the West Coast, and on the Wairau River in Blenheim. In 1967 *Nereid* was given a new 283 ci Chevrolet V8 motor, which gave her a top speed of 47 mph. This was the year Wesley won the coveted Raglan Cup. He continued racing until 1970 and sold the boat to a family member in Christchurch in the early 1970s.

Many years later, sons Les and Jeff have tried to trace her, but without success. It appears the original *Nereid* has disappeared without a trace. They are still searching for her, but, in the meantime, they decided to build a replica. The late Jim Boyd suggested he could build a hull off the photos that Les and Jeff had. He made a fantastic job of the reproduction. Many parts and components had to be handmade, as replica parts are not easy to find. The construction of the hull was in double-planked aspen poplar (grown and milled locally in Stoke) over black poplar frames. Wesley's grandson, along with Glen Nuttal, did all the engineering on the boat, which is powered by a 350 ci Chevrolet V8 motor.

The new *Nereid* was launched a day before the March 2015 Antique and Classic Boat Show and Regatta on Lake Rotoiti at St Arnaud. It was a very special day for the family with brothers, sisters, nieces and nephews in attendance.

She is a faithful reproduction of the original and has brought back many memories for the spectators and fellow boaties who recalled the original *Nereid*. She even took part in the organised race!

Renaissance

1948 replica

Owner Chris

This stunning 21-foot (6.4 m) mahogany speedboat looks as if she has been imported from America. Not so. She is a New Zealand home-built model. A one-off!

Chris's dad was a boat builder and Chris decided that he needed to get one of his dad's boats before he retired. Chris and one of his dad's staff undertook the build. Originally, Chris had in mind a knockabout boat, based loosely on a Pelin. Somehow the plans and ideas grew, and *Renaissance* is the end result! Six-metre sapele mahogany planks were imported from West Africa for the build. They are laid over kahikatea frames. To keep the power plant in keeping, a 1947 six-cylinder Chrysler side-valve flathead motor was found, done up and connected to a BorgWarner gearbox. She has a top speed of 30 to 34 mph. All the fittings were carefully selected and sourced, along with period-correct upholstery, to give the boat its overall retro look.

There is no doubt that this boat is a showstopper. Not only is she unique, but also stunning to look at. She's a boat that had non-boaties drooling, not to mention actual boaties. The fully varnished boat is complemented by a front double cockpit, fitted with two bucket seats and a step-through to a bench seat, all beautifully upholstered and making her an extremely practical boat for moving around on. Behind this, an extended deck covers the motor and then opens to another cockpit at the rear of the boat. The stern deck supports a flag pole, flying the New Zealand ensign. In the water the boat looks just as fantastic as she does on the trailer.

Vanquish

2012 (1930s plan)

Owner Dave

Vanquish is what is known as a 'gentleman's racer' of the top order. These boats were popular in the 1930s and '40s and generally featured a very long quarterdeck, with the two-seat or four-seat cockpit at the aft end of the boat. The motor was housed in front of the cockpit and was usually a straight six.

Vanquish was based on a design by Atkin & Co. (US). Started in 1906, the company specialised in producing boat plans for the amateur builder. These plans are still available from the original owner's widow. Dave, the owner of *Vanquish*, had the plans modified by a New Zealand naval architect.

Dave built the boat himself in a shed at home. The construction of the hull was in conventional marine plywood on a solid timber frame. Double bias fibreglass cloth covered the hull, which was then sanded, faired and painted. The deck is solid mahogany on ply. All the fittings and hardware were acquired with attention to period detail, as was the engine choice and the boat's layout. She is powered by a Ford 250 straight six (4.1 litre) and hooked up to a Paragon 1:1 forward/reverse gearbox. *Vanquish* tops out at 30 knots and her overall length is 19 feet (5.8 m).

Construction took place over seven years, and as time and materials allowed. Assistance with the project was received from the naval architect (plans), a marine engineer (motor installation), and a mechanic and several friends provided additional advice during construction.

I have admired these types of boats since reading about them in 1950s American boat magazines. Dave has made a stunning job of building his dream boat, so much so that it looks like a very fast boat even sitting on its trailer. In the water and under speed, she looks fantastic and certainly attracts a lot of attention.

Suzie

1935

This beautiful speedboat began her life around 1935 and is a Chris-Craft design, built in New Zealand. The boat arrived in Bruce's family when Jack (Bruce's father) and a partner, Francis Anson, purchased her from the previous owner. The solid kauri boat came minus a motor. Jack and Francis bought an ex-army Bren gun carrier that a neighbour had been using for mole ploughing. They took out the motor — a 21-stud side-valve V8 — and dropped it into *Suzie*. The families used the boat at Paraparaumu Beach each year — mainly for waterskiing — along with the odd trip to Kapiti Island. They also used her occasionally on the Whanganui River.

Around 1965, Jack's boys, now teenagers, revitalised the boat, renovating *Suzie* by fibreglassing the bottom and giving her a general tidy-up. The boys all learned to waterski behind *Suzie* at the beach, the river and also on Lake Taupo.

In the 1970s, eldest son Ken used the boat for three or four years, before buying a jet boat. *Suzie* was taken back by the other partner, Francis Anson. She lay out in the weather for some time before the farm where she lay got sold, so a friend, Loisie, took it to his residence rather than see the boat disappear. When Francis passed away, Loisie had no idea who the boat should go to.

Current owner Bruce started making enquiries about *Suzie* and eventually tracked her down. He had discussions with Francis's brother Jim, and Loisie, to see if he could reclaim the boat with the idea of restoring her. Bruce took her home where she sat in the garage for 12 years, before he decided that he had better restore her before he himself passed on.

Bruce and Margaret began the restoration, but decided the job was too big for them. They took her to Neville Rhodes, a cabinetmaker in Marton. The boat was again missing a motor, but Bruce just happened to have a 305 Camaro motor lying in the shed so this was installed in *Suzie*. Everything else was kept original: direct drive, press-button start and hand throttle. The old motor gave the boat a top speed of 32 mph, and the new motor does 40 mph.

It is still used as a ski boat and runabout.

Razzleberry

1948

Owners ◄ Richard and Rachel

Yep, she's a Yankee, but what a boat! Out of the factory in 1948, this Chris-Craft Deluxe runabout was delivered to a yard in Syracuse in February 1948. The Kiwi owner even has the original shipping slip. At 17 feet (5.2 m) in length she was one of Chris-Craft's most popular models and 1880 of them were produced post-war till the late 1940s.

The standard engine was a 220 ci straight-six, flat-head Hercules K-series engine, producing 90 hp.

Razzleberry is one of a small handful of sportier versions, featuring the 131 hp Hercules KBL engine. The extra horsepower was produced by increasing the engine displacement to 236 ci and adding triple carburettors. *Razzleberry* still has her original engine, which runs beautifully and, according to the owner, sounds like a Merlin aero engine when in full flight. Top speed is 45 mph, with a cruise speed of around 25 mph.

Richard bought *Razzleberry* in 2008 and imported her into New Zealand. Prior to that she was owned by a family that had a summerhouse at Greenwood Lake, Connecticut, New York, which is where the boat was used.

On arrival, the boat required some minor cosmetic work: the deck was re-caulked, the hull re-varnished and the bilge repainted.

The owners have had some memorable holidays over the past five to six years on all of the Rotorua lakes. They say that due to the small windscreen you can get a bit wet in rough weather, but the ride is excellent.

The owners reflect that riding in *Razzleberry* transports its crew back to a slightly less complicated age and when in her they all feel a little bit special and very lucky!

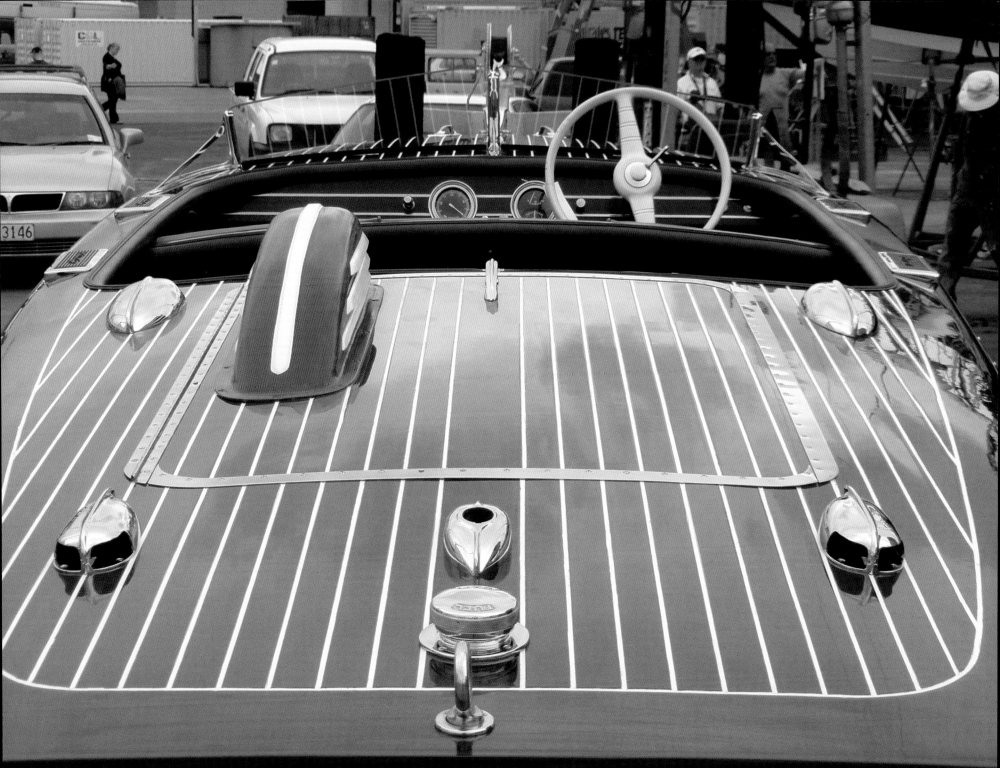

Calliope

1951

Owner Sven

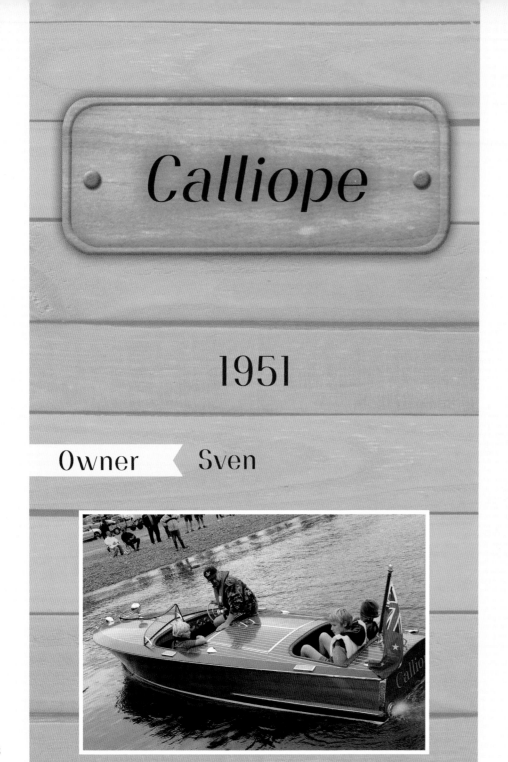

This beautiful example of a 1951 Chris-Craft design was only relatively recently imported into New Zealand by owner Sven. The boat is powered by an original six-cylinder Hercules motor, which has a capacity of 336 ci and develops 158 hp. It is mated to a Paragon 1:1 gearbox. The boat has a top speed of 45 mph.

These 19-foot (5.8 m) racing runabouts first appeared in 1948 and for the first two years of production were painted, as opposed to previous Chris-Craft models, which had a standard varnish finish. In 1950, the racing runabout models reverted back to mahogany and varnish. These boats were the 'hot rods' of the water and were easily the fastest Chris-Crafts available until the arrival of the 283 ci 185 hp V8-powered boats.

Calliope spent most of her life on Lake Weston in Connecticut. She was restored in 2006 and came second in her class at the Lake Tahoe Classic Boat Show in 2008.

This is a stunning example of a restored Chris-Craft boat. She has amazing varnish work on the hull and the deck is just beautiful. Both cockpits have been re-upholstered to the highest standards, and the detail around the motor is impeccable.

The American speedboats I have seen are, without exception, all amazing craft and really stir the blood just looking at them, let alone seeing them under way. They are a picturesque reminder of an elegant time past, where beauty, form and style ruled. They are the beautiful classic car or stunning hot rod of the lakes and sea. The owners of these boats can be justifiably proud of them.

Blondie

1948

Owner   Bruce

Blondie is one of the most handsome boats I have ever cast my eyes upon. The lines are perfect for what she was designed for and the use of blond and dark timber contrasting on her deck, combined with the mahogany hull, all beautifully varnished, make for a very pretty boat. Combine that with the deck layout, the expensive car-like upholstery, the fantastic dashboard and the attention to the period fittings, and you have a boat that is hard to walk past without stopping and going 'Wow!'

Chris-Craft runabouts and speedboats were all the rage in America after World War Two and the queen of the fleet was the 20-foot (6.1 m) Custom, produced from 1946 through to 1949. It introduced the blond two-tone deck design, along with all-new streamlined hardware. It also featured an expensive curved transom, referred to by Chris-Craft as a 'bubble' transom, and had rich leather upholstery. These models were powered by a Chris-Craft 283 V8 engine, developing 185 hp. It came with a Paragon 1:1 forward/reverse gearbox and had a top speed of 45 mph. Because of their size, weight and ride quality, they were often referred to as 'the Cadillac of the water'.

Of the 366 made, less than 25 per cent of them remain today.

Blondie was restored about 10 years ago and spent most of her life in the state of Vermont, in the US. She was imported into New Zealand in 2011.

Bruce offered to take my wife, Marilyn, and me for a spin. It was too good an offer to turn down. I found the boat to be incredibly stable and comfortable. It handled tight turns at full speed with aplomb, and was a joy to ride in. The smiles in the photo (see page 165) say it all.

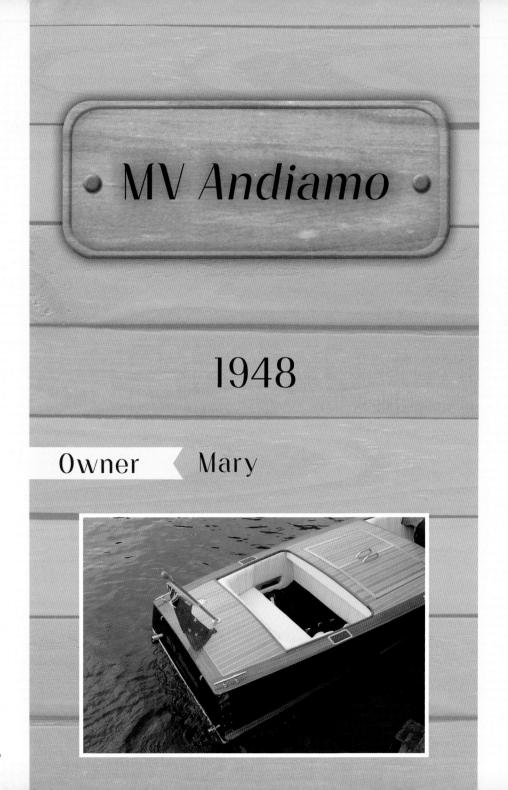

MV Andiamo

1948

Owner Mary

In 1948 this boat cruised the waters of Lake Rotoiti (North Island) under the innocuous name of 'The Yellow Boat'. She was built by a farmer in the Gisborne region and carried the honour of being the fastest boat on the lake, with a top speed of 42 mph. The speed was attributed to its Dodge straight-six engine and the classic-shaped hull.

In 2008, current owner Mary saw the boat advertised for sale as a virtual wreck for $900. Something about her beautiful classic lines cried out to Mary so she bought it. The hull had definitely seen better times, but Mary could see the potential to save and restore a piece of New Zealand maritime history. Son Rick got the restoration job and, over the next four years, restored the boat on a part-time basis, no doubt under his mum's eagle eye.

The interior of the hull was gutted and all the internal framework was renewed, simultaneously doubling its strength. New full-length engine bearers were fitted, and significant areas of the hull were replaced where dry rot had set in. All the timber work was done in kauri, in keeping with the original build. The hull was then fibreglassed, faired and painted.

The decking was done with a mahogany surround, a New Zealand kauri inlay, highlighted with kahikatea. Each individual piece was handcrafted to fit. For the deck, a supplier was found who could provide planks milled from a single tree so that a beautiful consistency could be maintained. Along the way a piece of stunning heart kauri was found in the timber supplied and this was kept for the dashboard.

When re-powering the boat, Mary was influenced by her husband, Wayne (a keen jet boater), and a 275 ci V8 motor was installed, delivering 280 hp through a BorgWarner gearbox.

The boat is now somewhat faster through the water than she was in 1948 and, believe me, Mary is not afraid to power her up. MV *Andiamo*, as she is now proudly called, is a gorgeous-looking boat and is a real credit to Mary and son Rick. This is a boat that really gets up and boogies. She is fast.

M.V. Andiamo

LAKE ROTOITI

Miss Tahoe

1966

Owner ▶ Phillip

This 19-foot (5.8 m) Century Arabian is one of the last mahogany-hulled boats produced by Century, before the company moved to fibreglass hulls. Some of the opposition had already moved to fibreglass and, in an effort to modernise their boats, Century fitted copious amounts of vinyl to the decks and upholstery. They were noted for their lounge pads over the engine hatches, providing a rear sundeck. (This upholstery styling is quite reminiscent of some of the sport saloon cars the Americans were producing at the time.) There were only 11 mahogany Arabians built in 1966, so this is an extremely rare boat.

When Phillip, the owner, was back in the States he visited the dealer he bought the boat from. While there, he met a man who was trying to trace his parents' boat, named *Miss Tahoe*. Subsequent conversations seemed to suggest that Phillip could have the very boat in New Zealand. On Phillip's return to New Zealand, a parcel of fittings from the boat arrived from the man he'd met in the US, along with a key. The letter stated that this was the spare key to his parents' boat, and that all the keys had been individually cut for these boats. He said if it fitted and started the boat, it would prove conclusively that Phillip had his parents' old boat. Phillip put the key in and turned it. Yes, you guessed it, the boat fired up (the boat runs an original Ford Intercepter V8 for a power plant).

Phillip has now become good friends with the American, who came to New Zealand to go out, once again, on *Miss Tahoe*. What a cool story and a wonderful reunion!

CF 3650 HW

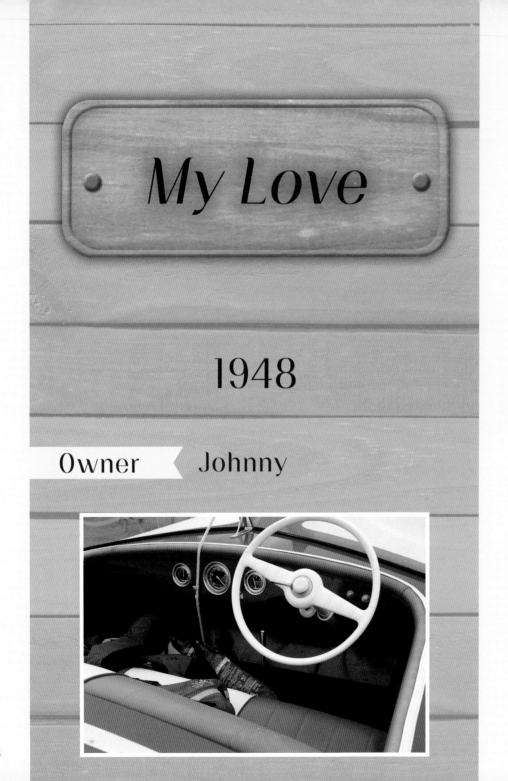

My Love

1948

Wellingtonian Johnny was trying to win his wife around to the idea of building his dream boat. She wasn't keen on another build and persuaded him to buy one instead. After researching online he found a Chris-Craft that suited his needs. Unfortunately, it was very expensive. Then came the global financial crisis, and classic boats in America halved in value. Then the New Zealand dollar rose against the US dollar. It was time to move and Johnny made his purchase.

The craft he bought is a Chris-Craft 19-foot (5.8 m) racing runabout, hull number 35 of 205 originally built. Although deemed a 1948 model, she was actually constructed in 1947 at Chris-Craft's Michigan factory in the US. She was shipped to her new owner in New York in September of that year.

Construction of the hull was originally Spanish cedar planking and mahogany frames. The hull has been rebuilt using some of the original planking and frames, using the West system resin base.

She is powered by an original 148 hp Chris-Craft marinised ML Hercules Motor Company engine. These engines were built during World War Two for use in US troop carriers and bought by Chris-Craft to convert for marine use. *My Love* has a top speed of 45 mph.

Owner Johnny imported her in 2009 from upstate New York, where she had resided for most of her life. He absolutely loves this boat, and loves taking people for a ride in her. As soon as he found out I was writing a book on retro boats, I was invited for a ride and whisked around the bay in this lovely boat. She is a little unusual for a Chris-Craft in that she has an attractive paint finish rather than the more traditional varnish.

Little Fliers

While researching speedboats, I found to my delight that there was something of a renaissance in the restoration of small speedboats and hydroplanes of 13 feet (4 m) and under. In fact, I started my powerboat career in such a boat (see photo of *Sea Witch* opposite). These small boats are fantastic and being so little feel very fast and exciting at speed. The boats featured here are the *crème de la crème* of the small boats I found in my travels.

The boats took me back to my early days with *Sea Witch*. After I had bought and restored *Canta Libre* (see page 114), I started to look at *Sea Witch*, which had already changed colour from purple to maroon and been renamed *Jezebel*, and I wondered what she would be like powered by an outboard. So I committed the great sacrilege (in hindsight) of ripping out the motor and re-decking her, and

strapping a brand-new outboard on her transom. I removed the skeg from the bottom of the hull and shaped a small wooden full-length keel and fitted it.

The test run was awesome. She hit 42 mph in a straight line, 5 mph faster than her inboard configuration. The problem came when I tried to turn. The boat turned fine, at least the hull did, but we kept going straight ahead at full speed sideways! Not quite as successful as it could have been. I look back now and think what an idiot I was to change her from the twin-cockpit configuration she had, but in those days she was just a cheap old speedboat and I was young and a total speed nut.

Fortunately, these little boats featured here all handle as well as *Sea Witch* did in her original configuration, if not better, and are a joy to watch at speed.

Dutchie

1955

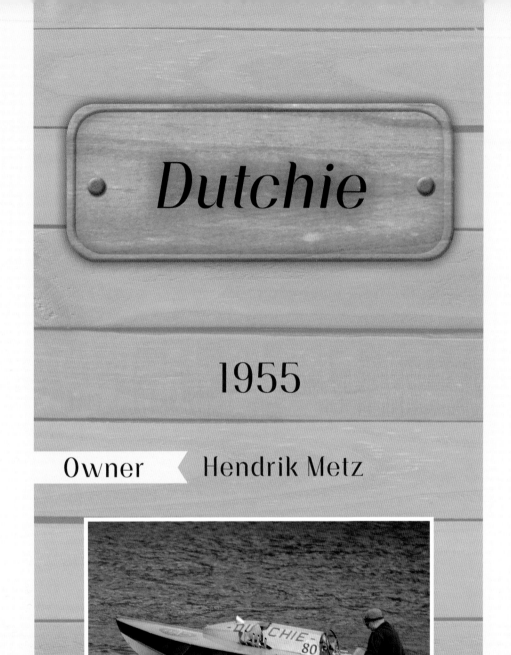

This little racing boat has an amazing history and has been in the same family for all her life. When I first saw her I was totally smitten with her. She obviously had a pedigree, and looked to be a pure racer like the ones I used to watch on the Waikato River in the mid to late 1950s.

Owner Hendrik was kind enough to forward *Dutchie*'s history to me. It was so eloquently written that I asked Hendrik whether I could use his words to describe this amazing little boat. So with his kind permission, here is some of *Dutchie*'s story:

The Metz family emigrated from the Netherlands to Wairoa, Hawke's Bay, in December 1950. Evert Metz Senior had been an avid amateur boat builder in the Netherlands and his passion for boating and sailing continued in New Zealand. Over his lifetime he built many boats, which included numerous dinghies, small yachts, houseboats and a number of speedboats, which his sons raced. One of their first speedboats was a small midget racer called Junior, *which was very successful in the 72 ci class, in spite of being unstable in rough water. It was decided that in order to be competitive, a boat of at least 12 foot [3.7 m] was needed, with a beam big enough to withstand the longitudinal rough waves generated by the boats, which kept bouncing back from the river banks making a very confused wave pattern. They had studied the behaviour of boats rounding the buoys on the course and concluded that any boat would have to be able to turn on a sixpence.*

My grandpa (Evert Metz Senior) started sketching on the back of an envelope, and one might say that this was the birth of Dutchie. Grandpa started building the boat the following Monday. Graham Lindstrom gave him an old Ford 10 engine, which was converted by using parts from the Ford 8 out of Junior.

Four weeks later (25 March 1955), before the Wairoa regatta, Dutchie was launched in the river in front of the Metz house and was showing her potential when the bronze drive shaft snapped clean in half.

With the help of Jack Allen, who turned the taper on his lathe, they had the whole thing ready again for the regatta next day. During the first race the turning fin came loose and she was forced to withdraw for the rest of the day. The following Monday the engine was taken out and the fin was solidly bolted to the keel. At the next meeting, held in Clive about four weeks later, it looked as though she was taking revenge as she completely outclassed the opposition and, as a result, was taken out of the midget class and asked to race against the big boys in A class, where she was more than able to hold her own.

During her time Dutchie was one of the fastest midgets in the Hawke's Bay and Taupo regions. She was beaten only by boats using Coventry Climax or Jowett Jupiter engines, which were faster on the straight and so were able to pick up what they lost around the buoys, as Dutchie was supreme at rounding them and quite often pipped them there.

By comparison, a Carl Augustin hull driven by a 100 E Ford engine, complete with overhead inlet and side-valve exhaust, four Amal carbs, hot cam, and aluminium flywheel, although a good five miles faster, was no match at all and was solidly beaten because of Dutchie's turning ability and stability in very rough water.

After a racing career of about eight years her bottom stoved in during an all-in flying-start river race. To fix this, a sheet of ply was screwed over the top, which slowed her down considerably.

When Dutchie was retired she was lifted into the rafters of the workshop where she remained until she passed into my care around 1998. I have taken care in her restoration to preserve her, as much as possible, exactly the way she was in the 1950s. Her current engine is a much milder E98A Ford 10, fitted with a copy of the Greene: cam, the same magneto, induction and exhaust manifolds, Holley 94 carburettor, and a chopper propeller.

Babychamps

2004 (1950s plan)

Owner   Johnny

The Glen-L boats were a popular American design in the 1950s and were designed in plan form for the home builder. Many of the plans were available through the *Popular Mechanics* magazine, well-read and available in New Zealand during the 1950s. The Glen-L Squirt was one of the smaller designs.

When Johnny decided to build this boat he modified the plans, as allowed by the designer, by spacing the frames further apart to lengthen the boat to 11 ft 6 in (3.5 m). The planing surfaces were left exactly as per the plan, but the sheer/coaming line was changed to narrow the deck width, and more camber/curvature was built into the deck.

She was constructed from 6 mm Meranti ply over Fijian kauri frames. Deck construction was made from 6 mm mahogany planking over 6 mm Meranti ply with Sikaflex caulking. Norski 221 pre-thickened epoxy glue was used throughout, with all timber sealed with Norski timber sealer.

A two-pack epoxy paint was used on the bottom of the hull and the sides were finished with three coats of Dulux Maxiproof polyurethane.

Johnny built the boat in 2004, taking just 150 hours from start to finish. She is powered by a 1956 Mercury 20 hp outboard, which returns a speed of 22 mph.

When the family wants to go a bit quicker, they remove the Merc and strap on a 1992 Mariner 25 hp, which gives a top speed of 34 mph.

These are great little boats and since starting this book I have come across a surprising number of them.

Mrs Robinson

2014 (1950s plan)

Owner/Builder/Driver Oli

Have you ever been blown away?

Well, I was when I saw this beautiful little hydroplane that had just been built from a 1950s plan by a 14-year-old high school student.

As part of a school project to build a skim board, the plan grew to encompass this boat. Oli was supported by his school and his dad, Johnny, who financed the project. Oli managed to complete the boat in 228 hours.

To see him proudly racing the boat around the lake, then taking out a major prize at the St Arnaud Antique and Classic Boat Show, was pretty awesome. Oli is an inspiration to teenagers of just what can be achieved if you put your mind to it.

The boat's construction incorporates Fijian kauri frames and stringers, hoop pine ply for the main girders and hull skin, and Gabon ply for the decking. Norski 221 pre-thickened epoxy glue was used to hold the boat together, with brass screws installed at a few critical points. All timber elements of the boat hull were sealed with two coats of Norski timber sealer. Dulux enamel paint was used on the painted parts of the hull, and Dulux clear coat on the timber parts.

Oli had to write a report on his boat-building experience as part of his school project and it makes for interesting reading so, with Oli's permission, here is a condensed version of Oli's report on tackling such a huge project:

Learning to build a hydroplane

I chose this project because I've always wanted to learn how to build a boat. I suggested it to my dad and he thought it was a great idea. At first I was just going to build a Tiny Titan, but then I decided that the larger model might be more work but it would be safer and

cooler. The initial goal I set myself was to build a Jupiter hydroplane. I planned this through researching different types of hydroplanes and I talked to my dad for some advice. He was very excited about this project, so much so that he agreed to pay for my expenses. He also helped in ordering the materials I needed because I didn't know the first thing about who to call for supplies, but he is in the construction industry so he was very helpful in that sense.

My goal

By the end I will have a boat that can float and also have something I can be proud of and can use for years to come. However, my main goal was probably to learn to build a boat. This whole process has been one big lesson for me. At the start I wasn't even that confident about cutting a bit of wood using the electric saw so that was probably the main goal …

What made this goal challenging?

The main things were: the plans were from the 1950s and were extremely hard to read; some areas were so physically challenging I simply couldn't do them so I had to get my dad's help, e.g., scraping sealer; and staying committed to doing the project because at peak I

was doing about an hour a night every night for about six months.

I overcame these challenges by firstly reading through the whole plan so when I came to read the plans later I found the text more familiar. I also had a lot of encouragement from my dad, and I also had the radio going to make the experience more enjoyable on the whole. My specifications were:

1. It has to be a functioning boat by the end of the project.
2. It has to look good.
3. It needs to go fast.
4. I want to look back at the end of the project and be proud of what I have done.

Sources

I used many sources, such as my dad's classic boat magazines, Google imaging certain boats to get a better idea of what sort of boat and colour scheme I wanted, looking at all sorts of boat websites, especially Hal Kelly's site (he was the designer and original builder of the Jupiter hydroplane). I also asked many experts for advice. I also asked a family friend who is a very skilled graphic designer, and I received engineering advice from Dr David Prentice on alterations I made to the plans.

I received advice from Johnathan Bacon on what paint would work well and I also received help from Reid McDonald who was our supplier of epoxy glue and seals, and Ryan Clarke on plywood thickness and layers, which was important because my boat has heaps of layers.

Application of information

I found out I had a long shaft engine so I had to make the transom longer, which could have contributed to my transom snapping on the original test run. This has taught me to be very cautious when changing original plans. I also learned by looking at images what it could look like, which influenced my ideas on paint job layout and my metal colours.

Overall how did the information affect my approach to the project?

Nothing could prepare me for when I originally received my plans and I looked at each step and I realised how much there was that needed to be done. Honestly, every single tiny piece of information affected and shaped my approach to the project until I was at the end and I put the boat in the water and, after running for a bit, the transom snapped. If my approach was how it was at the start of the project, I would have been gutted and I probably would have shed a few tears, but by the end I was already 'battle hardened' to obstacles put in front of me. Yes, I was absolutely heartbroken about the boat but I just had to get on with fixing it and through the information I had gathered about solving problems I knew that was the right way to go about it.

Achieving the goal

I feel I have achieved my goals because it is a functioning boat, even though on my first test drive the engine stalled and, when I started it up again, the transom snapped because there was still a bit of throttle on and when I turned it back on, the engine started with heaps of rpm.

I cut the engine and after I was towed back I noticed the damage, which was that the transom had snapped. I have fixed it now and the transom is four times thicker and is so much stronger. The first test run still proved that it floats and that it goes fast. I feel it looks pretty cool, and I can also safely say that I have looked back on this project and realised how much work I put in and I am very proud of achieving the goal.

Reflecting on the project

I have reflected on this project many times and thought about what I have learned and how my knowledge has extended and I didn't realise I was doing it but I have learned so much. For example, at the start of the project I wasn't even that confident when I was screwing a screw because I was afraid I would ruin the boat, but now I don't give things like that a second thought. I have developed as a learner through going from the person who sees one big problem to the sort of learner who looks at the problem of building a boat and sees the 30 steps that need to be followed, and I think to myself 'I could easily do one step.' After I get that mindset, I just do the one step 30 times. And to be honest, that's probably the best advice I could give anyone. And also my dad's advice: 'It's only a stuff-up if you can't fix it.'

What have I learned about myself as a result of doing this project?

I have learned many things about myself and how I can last under intense pressure to get something done over about 10 months, and how I can motivate myself to really strive for attention to detail, and how I can solve problems that throw themselves at me. I also learned a lot about how I can cope with disappointment and not achieving what I wanted to, or redoing something over and over till it's good enough. I think I coped pretty well.

By Oli M

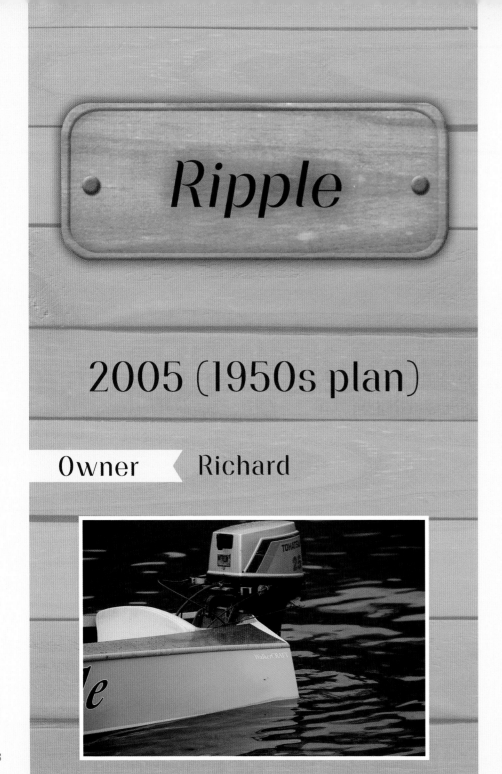

Ripple

2005 (1950s plan)

Owner Richard

The Snyder 12-foot (3.7 m) speedboat was built in Invercargill in the late 1950s, primarily as a family runabout cum racing boat. Five were built at this time. There is believed to be one left in original condition somewhere in Invercargill. Richard, the owner of *Ripple*, is a boat builder and had a hankering to own such a boat. He heard that there was one of the Snyders available for sale in Invercargill and drove down to have a look. The hull was a mess, but good enough to take decent patterns off. He bought the hull, took it back to his boat shop, patterned it and built an exact replica.

Over the years he had stowed away some exotic timber that had come his way and decided *Ripple* would be a good project to use it on. Native wineberry was used on the stringers, with the bottom stringers beefed up to strengthen the bottom of the boat. Non-native broom was used for the knees and around the seats, with Gabon ply used on the hull and decks. The quarterdeck was line-grooved to give the impression of a planked deck.

Richard initially powered her with a mid-'70s 25 hp Johnson outboard, and launched *Ripple* in 2005.

An opportunity arose to purchase a later-model propeller-rated 25 hp Tohatsu outboard, so Richard bought and fitted the motor to *Ripple*. He runs two propellers that he can interchange. The standard propeller gives her a respectable 35 mph top speed. With a racing propeller on she can achieve an amazing 44 mph. I suspect it feels a lot faster than that in this wee boat.

Ripple is a little cutie and reminds me a lot of the Glen-L Squirt model. These little fliers are an enormous amount of fun to use and are great for kids to learn boat handling and safety skills in.

Skinny Boat

1952

Owner Ross

This speedboat was designed and built in England by Albatross Marine (1949–66), a company created by two engineers: Peter Hives (son of Rolls-Royce director, Lord Hives), and Archie Peace (a Bristol Aeroplane Company aeronautics engineer). The first Albatross boats were built using war surplus aluminium. Approximately 800 were built and owners have included the likes of Stirling Moss, Brigitte Bardot, George Formby, Prince Rainier of Monaco, Prince Phillip and John Pertwee. Measuring 12 ft 9 in (3.9 m) in length and built in aluminium, several Albatrosses were imported by New Zealand agent Campbell Motors (Auckland) from 1951 through to 1956.

Many of these little speedboats were put into hire fleets on the lakes around New Zealand and were considered the MG Midget of the water. Generally powered by a Ford 10 motor, they were capable of around 33 to 34 mph.

Skinny Boat is a 1952 model and has lived all her life on Lake Rotoiti. She was built for Sir William Stevenson, the second mayor of Howick, and a well-known Auckland industrialist and philanthropist. His family owned *Skinny Boat* through till 1990.

Skinny Boat has a very advanced aluminium design for her time. For the 1950s they were light years ahead of anything else being built in aluminium. They had a twin-cockpit layout, and were a very pretty-looking boat. They are fast, nimble, and have excellent handling capabilities. They are also relatively cheap to run and simple to maintain.

The Albatross has held classic status for many years and is considered now as a collector's item throughout the world. There are at least three surviving restored sister Albatross boats in New Zealand. The others are *Albie*, built in 1955, *Mickey Mouse*, built in 1956, and *Little Fizzy*, built in 1951, all of which reside in Rotorua.

Having built aluminium runabouts in the '80s and having a natural interest in this type of boat, I was totally intrigued with their design. I had never seen this brand before so I'm very pleased to be able to feature *Skinny Boat* here, and capture this little bit of Kiwi maritime history.

From Propeller to Jet

Jet boats first appeared in New Zealand in the 1950s. They became more popular in the '60s and even more so in the '70s. When you think of jet boats in New Zealand you tend to think of well-known Christchurch company HamiltonJet, manufacturer of small recreational jet boats. But when they began, there was another company, Nalder & Biddle, manufacturing jet units.

The following three boats featured here trace those early days of jet boat development in New Zealand.

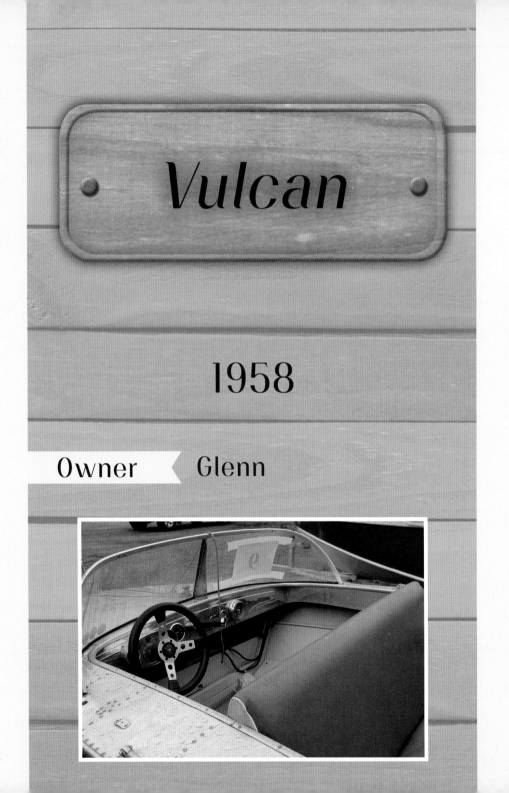

Vulcan

1958

Owner Glenn

This little boat grabbed my attention when I saw her parked on her trailer among a number of other classic trailer boats. She was built to the Glen-L Eldorado design, which was another late-'50s design with plans available to buy through the *Popular Mechanics* magazine. The American Glen-L designs were prolific. The main models built in New Zealand were the 10-foot (3 m) Squirt, the 14-foot (4.2 m) Swift and the 16-foot (4.9 m) Eldorado. The latter two were virtually the same in looks. They were notable for their 1950s-influenced rear tail fins, styled along the lines of the American cars of the same era. Quite a few were built in New Zealand during the 1950s and '60s.

What is different about *Vulcan* is that she was built in aluminium, as opposed to the more common build in marine ply. The topsides were even pop-riveted like a caravan. The hull is bare aluminium. As if this is not enough, she is also powered by a jet unit. Apparently, she was the brain child of a well-known tapware manufacturer in Nelson by the name of George Topliss, and was home-built in a back corner of his factory in 1958. George was a talented man and designed his own jet unit, which became the prototype for the Nalder & Biddle jet unit (see page 192). When the original intake housing was damaged, a production Nalder & Biddle intake was simply substituted. During his time George also designed and made an estimated 100 to 150 model-sized steam engines.

Vulcan was built as a saltwater ski/runabout, and used mainly at Monaco and Marahau in the Nelson area. Her first motor came from a Norton motorcycle, followed by a Ford 10 motor, and, finally, a 1500 cc Mk 1 Cortina GT motor, which she still runs today.

She is a great little jet boat and I am totally intrigued with her, particularly in her role in the development of the jet boat industry.

Miss Isel

1960

Owner Ed

While on holidays at Lake Rotoiti (South Island) in 1976, Ed's parents, Harry and Natalie, bought this boat after seeing it tucked away in the corner of a maintenance shed where Harry was having a chainsaw fixed. He purchased it from two park rangers who had moved on from Nelson Lakes National Park. The boat went home to Christchurch and, after this, was used for fishing in the Rakaia River and taken back to Rotoiti for summer holidays. They named the boat *Miss Isel* after Isel House in Stoke, Nelson, the childhood home of Natalie.

Miss Isel was built in 1960 and powered by a Ford 100E motor. This was connected to a Nalder & Biddle two-stage jet unit, serial number 006, which was one of only 26 built. These units were developed from the Topliss jet prototype jet unit that still resides in *Vulcan* (see page 194).

At the same time CWF Hamilton Ltd (parent company of HamiltonJet) was producing its Chinook two-stage, axial-flow jet units with quite some success. Apparently, Bill Hamilton was not happy with Nalder & Biddle manufacturing and marketing jet units in competition, and went to see them. It would have been great to have been a fly on the wall during that conversation. The end result was that Bill Hamilton convinced Nalder & Biddle to become the Nelson agents for CWF Hamilton Ltd, marketing their full range of products. The Nalder & Biddle jet unit ceased production after unit 26.

It is unknown how many of these 26 units still exist, let alone run, which makes *Miss Isel* a very rare boat. Originally varnished, *Miss Isel* was later painted for ease of upkeep. In 1986, Ed and his brother replaced the 100E motor with a Mk 2 Zephyr motor, which gave the boat considerably more speed.

A year later, Ed and a friend almost sank her after touching the bottom at speed in the shallows of the Waimakariri River. After this incident she ended up upside down on her trailer and there she stayed for the next 13 years.

Ed began to restore her in May 2000 with the removal of marine plywood from the bottom of the hull. He replaced it with a 70 cm-wide strip down the centre. The jet intake block was replaced, as the original had partly rotted. The rest of the original ply was attached, and a second layer of marine ply was fitted over the bottom, then fibreglassed. The sides and deck are all original plywood and have been stripped and varnished. The interior was repainted, and seating reconstructed and upholstered. The Mk 2 Zephyr motor was replaced with a Mk 3 Zephyr motor of 1962 vintage. She was completed in 2006. Two years later she was awarded the CWF Hamilton trophy for Best Classic Jet Boat at the St Arnaud Classic Boat Show and Regatta.

Today, Ed still enjoys this great little boat that his parents bought all those years ago, and Harry and Natalie, now in their mid-eighties, still take a lively interest in her.

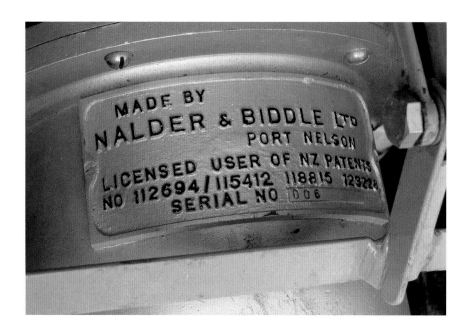

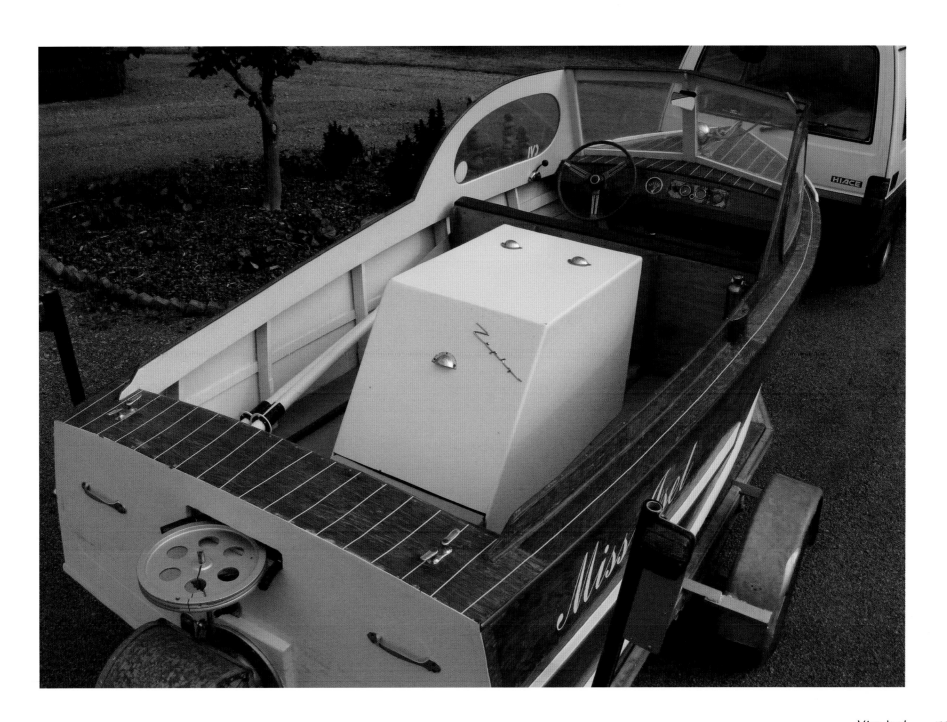

Hamilton Jet 30

1965

Owner Geoff

This little boat was among the first production boats built by Hamilton Jet Boats. Bill Hamilton, originally a South Canterbury sheep farmer, was an excellent engineer. From his home-based business he developed an excavator with an earth scoop, and later went on to build ski tows on Coronet Peak (1947) and Mt Ruapehu (1949). He moved his business to Christchurch in 1948, and in the '50s set out to build a boat suitable for the shallow braided rivers of the South Island.

Hamilton investigated the Hanley Hydrojet made in America, which drew in water and pushed it out through a steerable nozzle under the boat. A later modification, which put the nozzle above the waterline, proved more successful. The prototype jet unit was made in 1954, although it wasn't until 1956 that a reliable two-stage jet unit was built that could develop sufficient speed. On a return visit to the US in 1960 Hamilton took three of his jet boats, which became the first and only boats to travel up through the Grand Canyon. This trip took 2500 gallons of fuel and silenced Hamilton's many critics. He then went on to build his internationally successful business for which he is known today.

Geoff's Hamilton jet boat is one of the first production fibreglass jet boat hulls made, and is known as 'Jet 30'. Her length is 13 ft 10 in (4.2 m), and her beam 5 ft 10 in (1.8 m). The decks were built in marine plywood. She was fitted with a Hamilton single-stage Colorado Junior Jet unit, and is powered by a Ford 2.5-litre Mk 3 Zodiac engine. In their day, these boats would have been considered very advanced.

Geoff has owned this boat for some 18 years. When he bought her she was a bit tired so Geoff had the Zodiac engine fully rebuilt and also replaced the entire deck, again in marine plywood, giving it a varnished finish.

Since then the family has used it every summer for river boating, fishing and general boating. Geoff is now restoring a second jet boat, a Hamilton Jet 30 'XL', or at least that is what the family calls it. The 'XL' stands for 'extra long'. The boat looks identical to the original boat except for the fact that it is one foot (30 cm) longer. It is apparently one of very few built to this length. Geoff rescued this one from a shed in Hari Hari after a life on the West Coast, where it was used for deer recovery and, in later years, for getting to and from a whitebait stand on the Waitangitaona River.

The little Jet 30 looks great under power and is a great reminder of how revolutionary these jet boats were in their heyday.

Classic and Retro Launches

With a launch comes the exciting possibility of staying out on the water at night.
I was amazed when I realised how many classic launches inhabit the lakes and
coastal waters of New Zealand. They come in all styles, shapes and designs, and
some have very interesting histories.

They come from the South Island, the East Coast, the Hauraki Gulf, the Bay
of Islands, and from inland lakes. There are so many beautiful old launches that
I think I could easily write three books on them alone! I have chosen, though, to
showcase launches that come from lesser-known areas of the country, and which
are therefore less well known by the boating fraternity. I know the owners of these
launches are passionate about their own particular craft, and rightly so. They
deserve their moment in the sun.

Miss Kathleen

1902 or 1916?

Owner Barry

Supposedly a Logan launch, this beauty at 28 feet (8.5 m) is the redoubtable *Miss Kathleen*. Or is she? Redoubtable she surely is, but is she, in fact, a 1902 lady, or even a Logan? Sometimes the true history of these beautiful old launches gets lost in the mists of time, and the current owners can only go on what the previous owners have told them, unless they can find documented evidence to prove otherwise.

There is another view out there that *Miss Kathleen* might have been built by Aucklander David Reid in 1916. Her hull does not seem reminiscent of the Logan hulls, so perhaps the alternative view is correct.

However, there is no doubt that she was built in kauri plank, and that this displacement launch was originally built for a wealthy Whangarei family as a pleasure boat. She was well-known in the Bay of Islands for many years. Later, she spent some time as a commercial long-line fishing boat.

The current engine is a 30 hp David Brown and has been in the boat for over 50 years. *Miss Kathleen* underwent an extensive rebuild in 1989, and was purchased by the current owners from an old sea captain in 1997. She is a flushdecker design with an aft dodger cabin, meaning she has a flat foredeck with portholes in the side and a small stand-up cabin at the rear. The raised fo'c'sle and straight-stemmed bow give her that distinctive classic launch look that was quite a common configuration around the early part of the 20th century.

Viveen

1924

Owner   Andrew

When Andrew bought *Viveen* he was, as far as he was concerned, just buying a nice old boat that needed a little TLC. He had no idea that he had, in fact, purchased a bit of New Zealand maritime history. What he had actually purchased was one of legendary New Zealand boat builder Colin Wild's early landmark launches. Legend has it that Colin built a yacht when he was 18 years old and a launch when he was 19 years old. *Viveen* is reputed to be that launch.

She was built in Auckland in 1924 for a gentleman by the name of W Kapley from Devonport. *Viveen* was designed with the forward section featuring a reasonably deep 'V', and flattening out in the aft sections with a square-bilged planing hull aft. Her design showed influences of the latest John L Hacker American designs of the time. She started life with a 35 hp motor, which was later replaced with a higher-powered Winton motor.

Her owner raced her in the popular Auckland launch racing series (the Rudder Cup) until it died out in the mid-1930s. *Viveen* lived most of her life in Auckland before moving to Thames in recent years.

She has the ability, depending on the motor fitted, to show a fair turn of speed. One previous owner reported hitting 20 knots, with the throttle wide open in a following sea, coming back from Great Barrier Island. (Most people consider these old launches to be slow, but with the right horsepower motor fitted they could really move.)

When Andrew found her, her condition had deteriorated somewhat. He replaced the dodgy Ford 120 hp with a 77 hp Perkins diesel, rebuilt the stem, repainted the exterior and, even though he is using the launch, is now starting on an interior restoration.

Shortly after he bought *Viveen*, Andrew was contacted by the Auckland Boat Show to display her in an 'on the water' display of Colin Wild boats. The voyage up to Auckland from Thames was Andrew's maiden voyage in *Viveen* and all went well, if you can call battling 35-knot winds and rough seas as all going well! *Viveen* was taking green water over the bow and front cabin, but the trip gave Andrew a huge amount of confidence in her sea-keeping abilities.

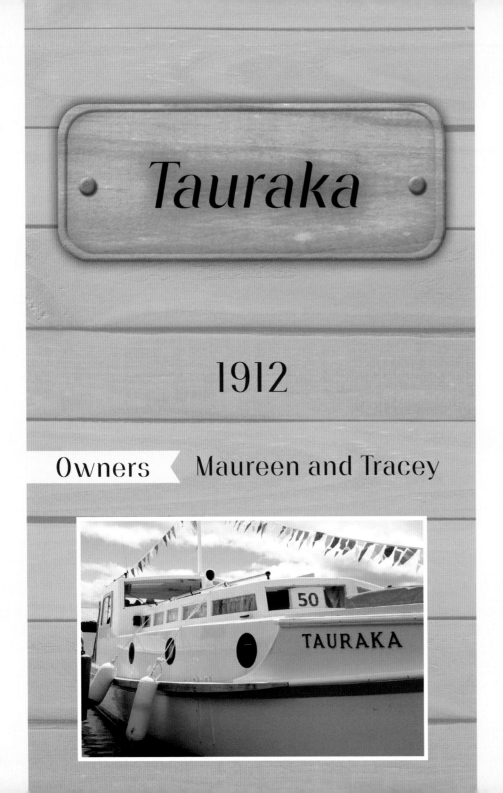

Tauraka

1912

Owners Maureen and Tracey

I have always loved the old bridgedeckers, flushdeckers and tram-top launches, so when I saw this old tram-top, I had to enquire about it.

The owners told me that this beautiful old launch was built and launched by Fred Mann for the new and very proud owner, FW Chalmers, in 1912. At the time she was a gaff-rigged sailboat with a 10 hp Frisco engine, and she went under the name of 'Helen G'.

Sometime around 1925 a family by the name of Carter from Tauranga bought her, owning her through to 1947. They renamed her 'Helen C'. The family had her modified to a single-mast motor launch, and the cabin structure was professionally altered to the tram-top and rear-dodger style she sports today. Her hull line is very typical of her build era and can be seen on many launches around New Zealand. At the time of the rebuild, she was residing in Tauranga.

When the family on-sold her she passed through the hands of another two owners, before being purchased by the current owners in 2005.

Tauraka is powered by a Fordson diesel engine. She now resides in Okawa Bay on Lake Rotiti, Rotorua, where the current owners enjoy cruising, trout fishing and joining in with the activities of the very strong Wooden Boat Association.

Arapawa

Thought to be 1932, now known to be much older

Owner ⟩ Mary

Arapawa is owned by Mary and is used regularly by Mary's daughter, Rachel, and husband, Warrick, for fishing and cruising. Both Mary and Rachel are very involved in the Wooden Boat Association.

The boat was built in 1932 and used in the Marlborough Sounds as a ferry to Arapawa Island.

She was brought to Rotoiti by Michael and Mary Taylor in 1996 and has been in every annual boat parade on the lake since they started. *Arapawa* measures 9.2 metres in length.

And that was the story, or so we thought. My enquiries about the history of the boat started Rachel off on a search, and she has since turned up some amazing stuff.

She tracked down some old-timers in the Marlborough Sounds, and one of them, Pete, wrote back saying that she was probably built by Ernie Lane in the early 1920s for a Mr Bay who started a guest house at Te Mahia. An old mate of Pete's thought she might have originally been called 'Gannet'. She was always distinctive due to the 'V' stern, and was the only boat like it in the Sounds. She apparently had a Bollinger two-stroke motor, which you had to stop then start it running in the opposite direction to reverse.

She was later sold to Tim Watson, who changed her name to *Arapawa*. He added a small wheelhouse then, later, got Jack Hansen to build a raised fo'c'sle head and new wheelhouse, which transformed her into a nice-looking launch. They also re-powered her with a new BMC motor in 1957.

She was later purchased by Des Tierney, who extended the wheelhouse and fitted a 75 hp Ford engine. He had her for 12 years before selling her to a Mr Jamieson.

A second letter arrived from Pete saying that an old friend had told him the boat was built in Titirangi, a bay in the outer Pelorus Bay. The current thinking is that *Arapawa*, formerly 'Gannet', could actually be 100 years old, dating from 1915! Pete has said he will try to confirm this by talking to old Jack Hanson, the boat builder who raised the fo'c'sle. He is now in his nineties and is probably the only man alive who can shed some light on this mystery.

It is very interesting when you start to dig into a vintage boat's past. Often what is deemed true history is really only a small part of it.

Marjorie Rosa

1930

This launch was built in 1930 by Sam Ford in Auckland, following a tram-top configuration with a flushdeck cabin and a raised companionway down the centre for headroom, joining into an aft dodger cabin open to the cockpit. She was used both as a pleasure boat and a fishing boat (for long-lining and catching tuna) in the Hauraki Gulf for most of her life.

The *Marjorie Rosa* came to Lake Rotoiti in July 2009 as a bare hull, with no engine or interior fittings at all. She had been completely gutted. Fraser turned her over to boat builder Tony Mitchell at Otaramarae. The plan was to retain the hull, which was very sound, remove the cabin top, and turn her into a bridgedecker, completely rebuilding the interior.

The interior was completed in New Zealand rimu, and one look confirms that no expense was spared in creating a stunning period-correct look. The cabin was constructed in oiled heart kahikatea and was beautifully made. As with the interior, there are many period-correct fittings and fixtures on the exterior of the boat, adding to the authenticity of the look and Fraser's vision.

The boat had no name when Fraser purchased her so he named her *Marjorie Rosa* after his mother, who despite suffering horrific injuries in a car accident was always a 'lady' in the truest sense of the word.

Marjorie Rosa was rebuilt to survey standards. Motive power comes from a 40 hp Lombardini diesel engine. The hull was painted in a dark green that sets off the topsides to perfection and certainly makes the launch stand out.

She was relaunched in 2013 and Fraser is enjoying his 'new' old lady immensely.

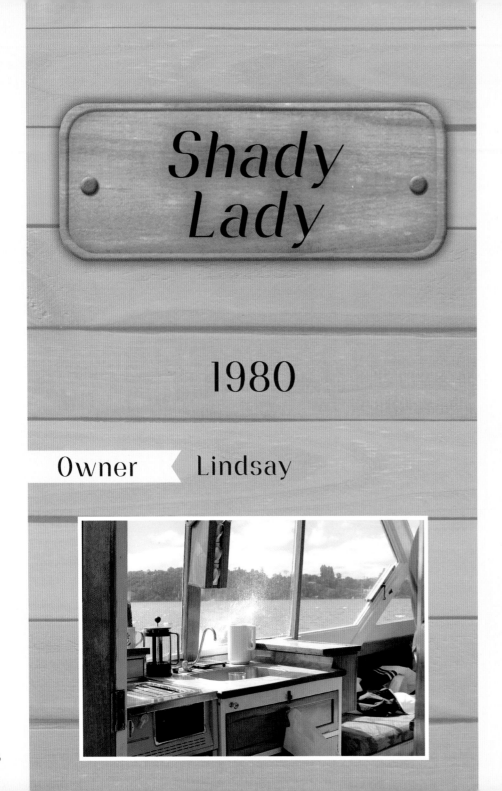

Shady Lady

1980

Owner ◀ Lindsay

Shady Lady was designed by Jim Young and is one of the Vindex line of boats. Jim Young, often referred to as the forefather of modern power boating in New Zealand, was a prolific designer, developing planing runabouts, cabin boats, trailer sailers, keelers, and the very successful Vindex and Formula range of planing launches.

Shady Lady is one of the first of the modern-type launches designed with a planing hull, and featuring large windows. At 27 feet (8.2 m), she was one of only seven built at this size. The best-known Vindex was the 32-foot (9.8 m) model. Of the seven 27-footers built, three were powered with 300 hp motors and were capable of top speeds of around 35 knots. The other four, including *Shady Lady*, were powered with much smaller horsepower motors and effectively became semi-displacement launches. In planing mode the boat would rise up and plane across the top of the water. A displacement boat is much slower and cuts through the waves rather than planing on top. In semi-displacement mode the boats tend to ride bow-up in a semi-planing displacement mode, sort of halfway between the two, with speed a little quicker than full displacement.

Originally named 'Relentless', she was in a collision with the Auckland Harbour Bridge. After that episode she was trucked to Lake Rotoiti and renamed *Shady Lady*. She regularly travels over 1000 miles on the lake each year and has attended all the Classic and Wooden Boat Parades since they started in 1998, making her a true 'lady of the lake'.

More recently Lindsay relocated to Waiheke Island, so the boat could be heading back to the Hauraki Gulf.

Whio

2005

Owner Peter

This launch was a surprise. At 29 ft 10 in (9.1 m), and sporting a very narrow beam, *Whio* has been trailered to both Lake Rotoitis: the one at Nelson Lakes, and the one at Rotorua. She is a lovely-looking, traditional launch that packs a heck of a surprise. *Whio* looks to have been designed and built in the early 20th century and beautifully restored with the utmost care and detail. Not so!

She was, in fact, designed by Peter, and built by Peter with the help of many friends and was launched in January 2005 at Coromandel. Boat designing must run in the family because Peter's dad, Ralph, designed and built a square rigger brigantine, *Breeze*, using traditional methods. Peter wanted a traditional-looking launch that was both fast and economical, and that he could easily trailer.

While I was cruising on *Shady Lady* (see page 216), I had been admiring Peter's beautiful displacement launch *Whio* nearby when, suddenly, he hit the throttle. The boat just took off, looking to be doing something in the region of 15 to 16 knots. It was the last thing I expected. I later found out that the easily driven hull has a slow-revving propeller hooked to a 50 hp motor. It is no problem to cruise at 17 knots and she can achieve 25 miles to the gallon cruising at 12 knots.

This is a beautiful and remarkable trailerable launch, and is an absolute credit to Peter. She certainly made a lovely sight the day I saw her. Peter has used her on inland lakes, both in the North and South islands, and, of course, in the Hauraki Gulf and beyond.

Rata

1926

Owner Steve

Rata is on only her second family of owners since 1936. Steve recently inherited her from his dad, Colin, who absolutely loved *Rata* and had completed a full restoration on her.

This launch has been a keel-up rebuild, carried out over a number of years. Nothing on this wonderful old launch has been left untouched. All the fastenings are silicon bronze. She is in pristine condition.

Rata was built by Dick Lang at St Marys Bay in 1926. Her length measures 35 feet (10.7 m) overall and she draws three feet (0.9 m). Her hull is kauri plank and she currently runs a Lees Marine Ford inboard diesel engine and cruises very economically at eight to nine knots. She apparently has quite a turn of speed at full throttle. The gearbox is a hydraulic BorgWarner set up. She is fitted with a good range of modern electronics, and has been domiciled in Thames for many years.

Rata sleeps five in three singles and one double berth, and is immaculate in the interior and very usable for extended cruising.

She is what is known as a tram-top launch, due to her rear cabin status with a centrally raised companionway running forward along the centre of the main cabin. The tram-style companionway gives standing room in the main cabin. She is a typical design of her era. Many happy family holidays have been had aboard *Rata*.

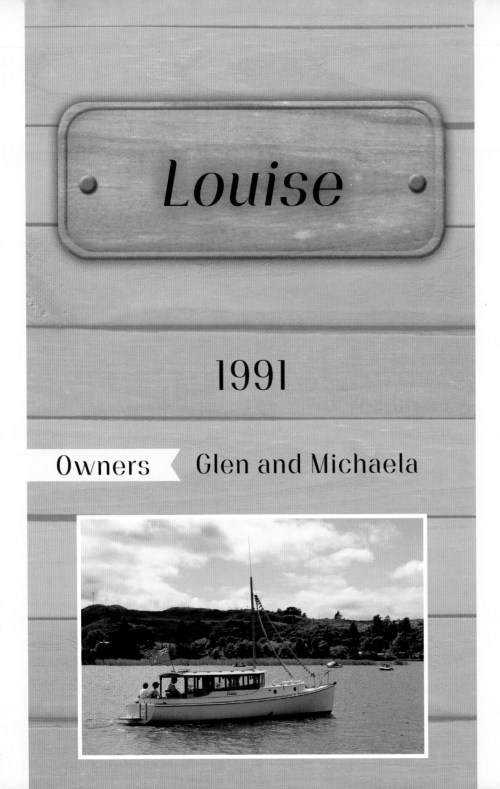

Louise

1991

Owners Glen and Michaela

Glen and Michaela have been residents of Okere Falls and had holiday homes on the Okere Inlet since 1993. As a family of six, now with adult children, they developed a desire to spend the small amount of quality time they had together doing something special. The general consensus was to buy a wooden launch that offered the style of boating the family enjoyed. The shortlist of requirements included style/looks, a social stern cockpit with helm station, a small galley, and berths for staying out overnight.

They had been looking for some time when Michaela and Glen saw an advertisement for *Louise*. They were both attracted to the boat and both independently thought, 'This is it.'

She was moored at Kawau Island's Bon Accord Harbour so Glen and Michaela travelled to Sandspit the next day and got the water taxi out and back. In the flesh, it fitted the bill perfectly and as Glen recalls, 'It was the first boat that Michaela made *me* buy!' (instead of the other way around). They paid a little more than the asking price to secure her, and had a boat haulage company transport her from Sandspit to Otaramarae. That was in 2012.

Louise had been at Kawau Island since 2000 where she was used for ferrying her then owner's guests from Sandspit to their home on Kawau, and for picnicking/fishing, etc. She was designed by Bruce Askew along classic lines, and built in 1991 by Calvin Berriman in the Bay of Islands.

Her construction is double diagonal kauri and glassed over. She measures 32 feet (9.8 m) in length, and carries a beam of 9 foot (2.7 m) and her draught is 2 foot (0.6 m). *Louise* is powered by a 35 hp Sole engine and has a top speed of approximately 7 knots, cruising at 5 knots. She has an Oregon mast with a steadying sail, a stern helm, and the cockpit has canvas and clears. There has been extensive use of kauri in the furniture and fittings, including a folding kauri table. She comes with four berths and a head.

I can quite easily understand how Michaela and Glen fell in love with this boat.

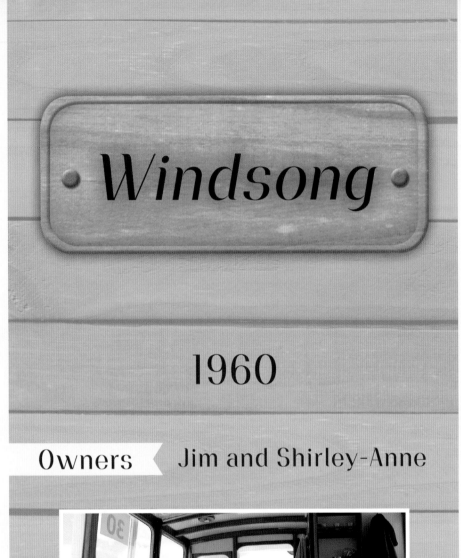

Windsong

1960

Owners Jim and Shirley-Anne

Windsong was designed and built by Shipbuilders Boat Company in Auckland. Her vital statistics give her a length of 8 metres and a beam of 2.9 metres. Her hull construction is double-skin mahogany ply, glassed over.

Powered by a Ford series four-cylinder diesel engine through a Paragon hydraulic gearbox, she cruises nicely at 7.8 to 8 knots at 1750 rpm, but has a maximum speed of 10 knots.

Legend has it that a number of these boats were built with materials left over from the construction of the navy's Fairmile motor launches built during World War Two, although it appears Shipbuilders was not involved or commissioned to build any Fairmiles.

Windsong underwent an extensive refit in 1978, including a new engine, glassing of the hull and a cabin refurbishment.

It appears that *Windsong* spent the majority of her life in and around the Marlborough Sounds. A Havelock owner had at one time owned her for 20 years. Jim and Shirley-Anne purchased the boat in Picton. She was sailed across Cook Strait to Mana Yacht Club in Wellington by a professional skipper, who commented that she had exceptional sea-handling capabilities. From Mana, she was transported by road to Lake Rotoiti, where she is used extensively for trout fishing and family cruising.

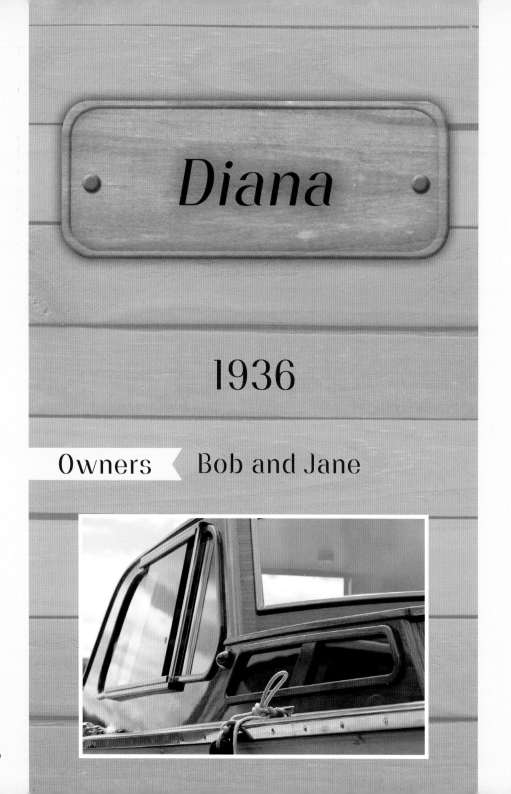

Diana

1936

Owners Bob and Jane

This launch was built in Suva, Fiji. The first owner had the surname of Ludolf, and was the chief engineer in Fiji's equivalent of New Zealand's Ministry of Works. The launch was originally called 'Ripalong', and it appears she may have been a John Atkins design, as the current owner discovered photos of a John Atkins design with the model name 'Ripalong'. The two boats look identical.

She was bought to New Zealand as deck cargo in the mid-1950s by the McGinley family, who had purchased her after World War Two when they immigrated to New Zealand.

Bob, the current owner, tracked down the McGinley family and found that they had been responsible for changing the launch's name to *Diana* (named for their eldest daughter). They said that while in Fiji *Diana* had been used as a patrol boat during the Queen's visit in 1953. On that occasion, her image was in the background of a photo taken of the Queen getting into a boat from the *Britannia* to go ashore at Fiji, and they were pretty sure it appeared in a *National Geographic* magazine. Bob went online to search for it, found nothing, and was just about to give up when he found it in a 1958 *National Geographic* some five years after the event. Bob has since found a hard copy of the magazine!

Diana resided in Auckland for many years, both in Devonport and up the Tamaki Estuary. During this time she was powered by a Dodge inboard motor and was reputed to have a top speed of 25 knots. At some stage she ended up on Lake Rotoiti and had resided there for some 18 years before Bob found her.

By that stage she had been sadly neglected and was pretty well a wreck. Bob instigated what was to be an almost full rebuild. The hull was extended and a false transom fitted. The 'hunk of iron' that had once been an engine was biffed and a 60 hp Mercury Barge outboard was fitted in front of the false transom. When the hull was extended it was found to be very close in looks to a Brin Wilson Boat Builders design, so when rebuilding the cabin they followed the Brin Wilson look.

Diana's hull was built in single-skin kauri and, during the rebuild, all the caulking was removed and kahikatea strips were splined in between the planks and the hull was glassed over. The topsides were done in both solid mahogany and mahogany ply, with the cabin top being moulded in a mahogany ply and foam sandwich.

Diana is now 28 feet in length (8.5 m), and has a beam of 8 ft 2 in (2.5 m). She has a flat bottom (excluding the keel), and draws 400 mm on the keel, with the rest of the hull drawing just 100 mm. She cruises at 15 mph and makes a beautiful 'lady of the lake'. The woodwork completed on the rebuild is exquisite with some of the curved areas looking particularly gorgeous.

Alberta

1913

Alberta was built in 1913 by HN Burgess Boat Builders to a flushdecker design. Her length is 28 ft 6 in (8.7 m).

Initially powered by a low-horsepower engine of around 8 hp, she was re-powered with a larger Scripps motor in 1914. The first owner was a Mr Parsons and, in 1918, she changed hands to the Palmer family.

A chap by the name of Maurice Williams owned her in 1959 and had her rebuilt, then on-sold her around 1961. She turned up moored in the Milford marina on the North Shore of Auckland.

Artie Perkins bought her in 1969 and re-powered her with, yes, you guessed it, a 36 hp Perkins diesel.

Andrew Campbell owned her in 2002 and she still resided in the Milford marina, and still had her flushdecker topsides. Over these years she was regularly seen plying the waters of the Waitemata.

Jon now owns *Alberta* and she has been fitted with a period-correct aft dodger cabin. He uses her for cruising and fishing.

Kotuku

1923

Owners Alec and Verene

This beautiful old launch is Rotorua born and bred.

Kotuku was built by the Robinson Brothers Boat Builders in Rotorua in 1923. She is 28 feet (8.5 m) in length and has a beam of 8 ft 6 in (2.6 m), and a draught of 2 foot (0.6 m). *Kotuku* is built in double-skin kauri. Having been on the lakes all her life she was at one point in time operating as a tourist launch out of Okawa Bay. At another time she was used for weed spraying around Lake Rotoiti.

Sometime in the 1930s she was purchased by Jack Bloomfield of Auckland, but *Kotuku* remained on the lake, passing through three generations of the family. At this stage she had a top speed of 15 knots and was sometimes seen towing waterskiers! That must have been a real sight to see.

Originally, she was powered by an Ailsa Craig marine engine that required cranking to start. In the 1950s she was re-powered with a Gray Marine six-cylinder motor and had a major refit of the cabin structure, moving from the original flushdecker design to a sedan launch.

The 1970s saw her sink in her boatshed after youngsters tampered with her. Fortunately, she was refloated with minimal damage.

In the '80s *Kotuku* was re-powered once again with a Volvo Penta 140 hp engine and, in 2005, local boat builder Tony Mitchell gave her a complete refit before relaunching her in the same year.

Kotuku has seen 93 years' service on Lake Rotoiti and is well-known by her nickname, 'The K'. The name 'kotuku' means 'white heron' and she was so-named after the white heron that frequented the Ohau Channel and Okawa Bay from time to time. These days, she still cruises and fishes on the lake, in the capable hands of Alec and Verene. She is without a doubt a lovely old launch with a rich Rotorua history.

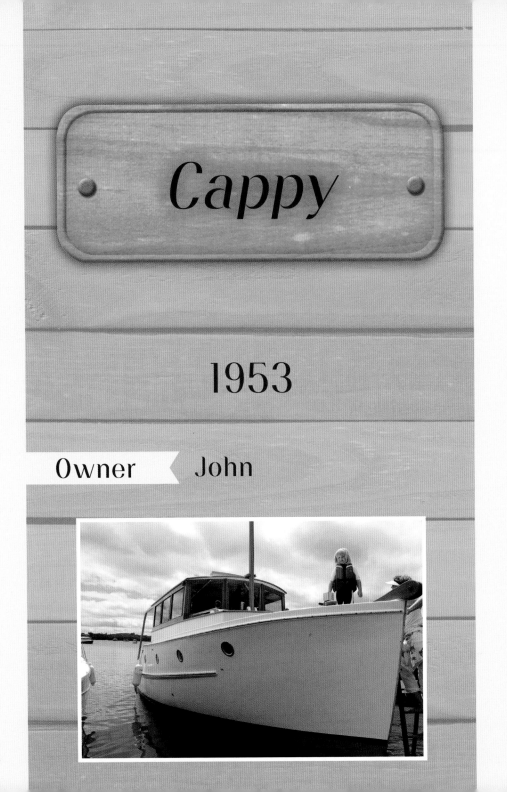

Cappy

1953

Owner John

This boat first saw the light of day in 1953. She is a Bailey design and her length is 8.5 metres.

Cappy spent her early life at Paremata and was owned by a Mr Roberts in the early 1960s. She was sold in the early '80s and, under the new ownership, became rather neglected.

A local boat builder by the name of Brian Billings picked her up in 1986 and she was relaunched at Mana after being completely rebuilt in a shed at Craters Edge. *Cappy* spent a short time at Napier before going to Waikawa, where, in 1988 and after some financial troubles, she was on-sold to Ron Spinks of Christchurch. Ron and a mate motored her down to Lyttelton. Purchased by Kevin Wild in 1992, she was altered to make her more comfortable.

With a wood-burning stove fitted, she was always the most popular boat for socialising in.

The current owner, John, purchased her in 1998. *Cappy* was trucked north to Tauranga where she was refitted at Peter Marks' boatyard before making her final journey to Lake Rotoiti. She is used for trout fishing and cruising the lake.

Achernar

1939

Owner Don

This was the only launch designed by RL Stewart, a well-known yacht designer of the time. It was built for his father by Collings and Bell, boat builders in Auckland. She is of kauri plank construction and measures 30 ft 10 in (9.4 m), with a beam of 9 ft 2 in (2.8 m).

When war broke out, *Achernar* was requisitioned by the navy, like so many other launches at the time. Late in the war, she ended up as the recreational craft for an American admiral by the name of William 'Bull' Halsey. The erstwhile admiral took a shine to the launch and renamed her 'Betty'.

After the war the admiral shipped the launch to the US but, fortunately for us in New Zealand, she was dropped and broke some ribs in Fiji en route. Subsequently, she was shipped back to New Zealand and assumed her original name of *Achernar*.

She had a number of owners post-war who resided, respectively, in Auckland, Tauranga, Thames and the Bay of Islands. In 1984, she was given a major refit and had a flying bridge added by the Lane Motor Boat Company.

Later in 1993 the gearbox and propeller shaft were replaced and the owner fitted a new motor, which was able to be lowered and moved aft to be accommodated under the rear seats in the cabin and the front seat in the cockpit.

When the current owners purchased her they had the flying bridge removed, and she was restored by Mike Lowe to as close as possible to her original shape and colour scheme. She has lovely lines and is so typical of the period she was built in. With the flying bridge removed, she has resumed her classical sedan-style cabin top. The varnish work is immaculate and she has a very user-friendly cockpit. The main cabin has the galley to starboard, with the helm station forward of that, and L-shaped seating to the port side.

Achernar is a great cruising boat and the current owners use her for both cruising and fishing.

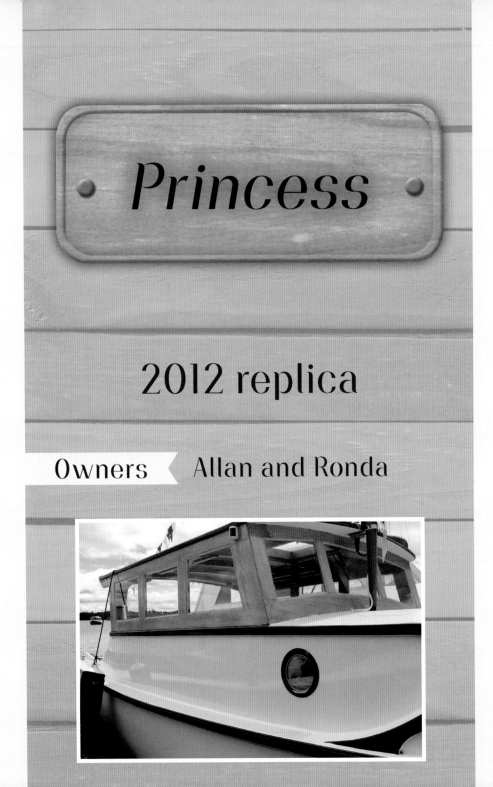

Princess

2012 replica

Owners Allan and Ronda

Some 40 years ago Allan bought an old launch that looked pretty similar to *Princess*. It was a bit of a dog and was pretty cheap to buy. It leaked like a sieve and, eventually, Allan stripped off any fittings of value, stored them away for a rainy day, and chopped up the boat for firewood.

Many years and many boats later, and as a member of the Rotoiti Wooden Boat Association, he offered a photo of the old launch to be used as the Association's letterhead. A good move, he thought, as no one's nose could be put out of joint since the boat no longer existed.

One day, a club member heard the story and said to Allan, 'You should never have chopped her up.'

Well, Allan took it a bit to heart so decided to design a replica of the boat and build it himself. He had a few other ideas he had seen on other boats that he liked, and so incorporated them into the design. He fossicked around in his shed and found a lot of the fittings from the old boat, such as ventilators, portholes and cleats, which were then fitted to his new build.

Princess is the result. She is a delightful-looking replica launch of yesteryear, and a credit to Allan's design and build skills. She is powered by a 28 hp Kubota diesel motor, cruises at 6 knots, and will carry six to eight people comfortably. She is just 22 feet (6.7 m) long.

More Beautiful Boats

Rafted up in Rotorua.

Tucked away in Thames.

Mucking about in Mahurangi.

A bridgedecker.

A sedan launch.

Out of the '50s — boats on the shoreline.

Old-timers in Taupo.

Choice classic trailer boats.

More trailer boats.

A classic hydroplane.

Acknowledgements

Books are seldom written without the input of other people, whether through advice, knowledge supplied, or photographs, and this book is no different.

I must acknowledge my wife and best friend, Marilyn, for taking on the task of official photographer for this book and making such a fantastic job of it. Eighty per cent of the images have been captured by her lens. I also thank her for her patience and advice on the script and her painstaking pre-edit proofreading.

My thanks must also go to my editor, Antoinette Sturny, whose input into this book, as well as my previous two books,

Retro Caravans: Vantastic Kiwi Collections and *A Great Indoors for the Great Outdoors: The Story of Liteweight Caravans*, has been outstanding.

Designer Cheryl Smith has also been great to work with.

Lastly, and most importantly of all, I would like to acknowledge Bill Honeybone, Publishing Consultant at David Bateman Ltd, who took me on as a raw author and has mentored me through these first three books. I am indebted to him for his guidance, patience, knowledge and enthusiasm.

Also by Don Jessen